I0426255

ISIL IN AMERICA:
DOMESTIC TERROR AND RADICALIZATION

HEARING

BEFORE THE

SUBCOMMITTEE ON CRIME, TERRORISM, HOMELAND SECURITY, AND INVESTIGATIONS

OF THE

COMMITTEE ON THE JUDICIARY

HOUSE OF REPRESENTATIVES

ONE HUNDRED FOURTEENTH CONGRESS

FIRST SESSION

_____

FEBRUARY 26, 2015

_____

Serial No. 114–6

_____

Printed for the use of the Committee on the Judiciary

Available via the World Wide Web: http://judiciary.house.gov

_____

U.S. GOVERNMENT PUBLISHING OFFICE

93–527 PDF   WASHINGTON : 2015

For sale by the Superintendent of Documents, U.S. Government Publishing Office
Internet: bookstore.gpo.gov   Phone: toll free (866) 512–1800; DC area (202) 512–1800
Fax: (202) 512–2104   Mail: Stop IDCC, Washington, DC 20402–0001

COMMITTEE ON THE JUDICIARY

BOB GOODLATTE, Virginia, *Chairman*

F. JAMES SENSENBRENNER, JR.,
  Wisconsin
LAMAR S. SMITH, Texas
STEVE CHABOT, Ohio
DARRELL E. ISSA, California
J. RANDY FORBES, Virginia
STEVE KING, Iowa
TRENT FRANKS, Arizona
LOUIE GOHMERT, Texas
JIM JORDAN, Ohio
TED POE, Texas
JASON CHAFFETZ, Utah
TOM MARINO, Pennsylvania
TREY GOWDY, South Carolina
RAUL LABRADOR, Idaho
BLAKE FARENTHOLD, Texas
DOUG COLLINS, Georgia
RON DeSANTIS, Florida
MIMI WALTERS, California
KEN BUCK, Colorado
JOHN RATCLIFFE, Texas
DAVE TROTT, Michigan
MIKE BISHOP, Michigan

JOHN CONYERS, JR., Michigan
JERROLD NADLER, New York
ZOE LOFGREN, California
SHEILA JACKSON LEE, Texas
STEVE COHEN, Tennessee
HENRY C. "HANK" JOHNSON, JR.,
  Georgia
PEDRO R. PIERLUISI, Puerto Rico
JUDY CHU, California
TED DEUTCH, Florida
LUIS V. GUTIERREZ, Illinois
KAREN BASS, California
CEDRIC RICHMOND, Louisiana
SUZAN DelBENE, Washington
HAKEEM JEFFRIES, New York
DAVID N. CICILLINE, Rhode Island
SCOTT PETERS, California

SHELLEY HUSBAND, *Chief of Staff & General Counsel*
PERRY APELBAUM, *Minority Staff Director & Chief Counsel*

———

SUBCOMMITTEE ON CRIME, TERRORISM, HOMELAND SECURITY, AND INVESTIGATIONS

F. JAMES SENSENBRENNER, JR., Wisconsin, *Chairman*
LOUIE GOHMERT, Texas, *Vice-Chairman*

STEVE CHABOT, Ohio
J. RANDY FORBES, Virginia
TED POE, Texas
JASON CHAFFETZ, Utah
TREY GOWDY, South Carolina
RAUL LABRADOR, Idaho
KEN BUCK, Colorado
MIKE BISHOP, Michigan

SHEILA JACKSON LEE, Texas
PEDRO R. PIERLUISI, Puerto Rico
JUDY CHU, California
LUIS V. GUTIERREZ, Illinois
KAREN BASS, California
CEDRIC RICHMOND, Louisiana

CAROLINE LYNCH, *Chief Counsel*

CONTENTS

ISIL IN AMERICA:
DOMESTIC TERROR AND RADICALIZATION

THURSDAY, FEBRUARY 26, 2015

House of Representatives

Subcommittee on Crime, Terrorism,
Homeland Security, and Investigations

Committee on the Judiciary

Washington, DC.

The Subcommittee met, pursuant to call, at 10:19 a.m., in room 2141, Rayburn Office Building, the Honorable F. James Sensenbrenner, (Chairman of the Subcommittee) presiding.

Present: Representatives Sensenbrenner, Goodlatte, Jackson Lee, Conyers, Gohmert, Chabot, Poe, Chu, Bass, Labrador, Richmond, Buck, and Bishop.

Staff Present: (Majority) Allison Halataei, Parliamentarian & General Counsel; Caroline Lynch, Subcommittee Chief Counsel; Jason Herring, Counsel; Alicia Church, Clerk; (Minority) Aaron Hiller, Counsel; and Veronica Eligan, Professional Staff Member.

Mr. SENSENBRENNER. The Subcommittee will come to order. Without objection, the Chair will be authorized to declare recesses during votes in the House. I will yield myself 5 minutes for an opening statement.

Today's hearing will examine the Islamic State of Iraq and the Levant, or ISIL, and the domestic terrorism threats posed by these terrorists. And while ISIL seems to have reared its head only in the last 18 months, a closer look quickly reveals ISIL to be an old foe; one with whom the United States has done battle for more than a decade. Before the group declared itself a global caliphate and adopted its current name, it was merely the Islamic State of Iraq. During war, members of this same group were among the most prolific perpetrators of attacks upon American troops and our partners in Iraq.

The procession of name changes; however, has made no difference at ISIL's commitment to harm Americans. Earlier this month, we were all reminded of this when we learned of Kayla Mueller's death after 18 months of ISIL captivity. The 26-year-old from Prescott, Arizona traveled to Syria with Doctors Without Borders to help alleviate the suffering brought there by Islamic extremism. Distance does not make us in the United States immune from ISIL's destructive ideology. From far beyond the battlefields of Syria and Iraq comes funding and support for this group's call to arms against the West, and the domestic threat is not limited to New York City and our Nation's capital.

Two weeks ago in St. Louis, five Bosnians were charged with providing material support to ISIL. The suspects allegedly provided weapons, military uniforms, and equipment and money to a sixth Bosnian who left the United States in 2013 to join ISIL and Syria. Alarmingly, all six individuals are natives of Bosnia who immigrated to the United States. Three are now naturalized citizens and the remaining three have either refugee or legal residence status. But the threats posed by ISIL's hateful ideology are not purely external. Inciting Americans to join their ranks or to ally their selves with ISIL's mission is a pivotal component in their campaign of violence against America and its people.

Last month, a Cincinnati man named Christopher Lee Cornell was arrested at a gun shop purchasing multiple weapons. He is alleged to have been collecting for an attack here in Washington, D.C. Mr. Cornell became an adherent of radical Islam on the Internet having adopted the Jihadi world of view. He aimed to gun down Members of Congress and government employees for the glory of ISIL, a terrorist group on the other side of the world with whom he had no connection except devotion to this same perverted Islamist ideology.

As FBI Director Comey has pointed out, these are not isolated incidents. ISIL's connections are being investigated in virtually every part of the United States, but on the heels of the St. Louis and Cincinnati arrests, in just days after ISIL released a video depicting the beheading of 21 Egyptian Christians in Libya, President Obama convened a summit on countering violent extremism. A summit that failed to include the FBI Director James Comey and refused to acknowledge that ISIL and other terrorist organizations are motivated by radical Islam.

As one commentator noted, the summit was strangely sympathetic to Islamic sensibilities in grievances at the very time when rampaging Jihadists, while quoting Islamic scripture, are barbarically slaughtering their enemies and conducting a pogrom against Christians.

The President's unwillingness to acknowledge the true motives of these terrorists, not only embolden stir campaigns of terror, it makes Americans less safe. Meanwhile, ISIL continues its march across western Iraq and continues to spew its propaganda of hatred and murder across the globe. Yesterday, three New York City residents, two from Uzbekistan and one from Kazakhstan, were arrested for plotting to travel to Syria to join ISIL and "wage jihad." According to the criminal complaint, one of these men stated he would kill President Obama if he had the opportunity to do so.

The witnesses today will hopefully shed light on the escalating domestic terror threat posed by ISIL and those who would ally themselves with Islamic extremism.

It is now my pleasure to recognize for her opening statement, Ranking Member of the Subcommittee, the gentle woman from Texas, Ms. Jackson Lee.

Ms. JACKSON LEE. Good morning.

Thank you so very much, Mr. Chairman, and thank you for holding this hearing. We are finding so much common ground as we try to include issues of criminal justice reform, but also securing the domestic tranquility of this Nation.

This hearing is involving ISIL in America, domestic terror, and radicalization. And so, it is important to note that this Islamic State is a brutal terrorist organization, it has murdered thousands of civilians including four United States citizens, it threatens to topple regional movements, it has, as its stated goal, the religious and ethnic cleansing of the areas under its control. But I think it is important to note, as has been said by our Commander and Chief, United States is not at war with Islam but it is the contorted, disjointed and ludicrous interpretation of those who simply want to be violent and vile and kill people.

And even if it cannot strike the United States homeland directly as it has been alleged, ISIL clearly hopes to inspire Americans to act against us from within. As evidence, the Chairman has already noted, there are three would be ISIL actors caught and apprehended by the FBI, in which I thank you so very much, two at John F. Kennedy airport where millions travel every day, as do millions every day in the United States; grandmothers going to see grandchildren, College students going home, business persons seeking to participate in the capitalistic system of this Nation, or people simply going to vacation maybe even in the Nation's capitol, the cradle of democracy for this Nation.

So while I am grateful that the United States is leading a multinational coalition to degrade and ultimately destroy Islamic State, I am certain that we cannot bomb our way out of this problem. In my view, the domestic threat posed by ISIL and other terrorist organization must be met on three fronts.

First, we must engage in real outreach to the communities most at risk for radicalization. By outreach, I do not mean the past practices of certain police departments that deployed undercover agents into mosques and community centers. Maybe the only approach, we know that is the approach that is used when you are investigating. Nor do I mean that the heavy-handed use of informants within certain immigrant communities. These tactics have been misdirected and costly.

Countering violent extremism should not ever be the pretext to profiling a United States person on the base of race, religion, or culture. However, we know that intelligence gathering is important. And so, I certainly believe that that is a strong element of making sure that those who want to do us harm do not do so.

But last week, I had the privilege of attending the White House Summit on Countering Violent Extremism. At that event, President Obama observed terrorist groups like al-Qaeda and ISIL deliberately target their propaganda in the hopes of reaching and brainwashing young Muslims, especially those who may be disillusioned or wrestling with their identity. The president is right: ISIL has proven adept at using social media to spread its message. The United States in near time calculates that the group posts 90,000 tweets and social media responses every day.

How do we combat this propaganda? By empowering local communities, teachers, faith communities, and police officers alike to talk openly and honestly about what ISIL is, what it threatens to do, and how it twists the basic threats of Islam to service its own purposes. I am particularly interested in how we can engage with segments of these communities that often go overlooked. For example, women and young people who are not always invited to participate in the dialogue that have the power to spread a positive message where police officers and government spokespersons cannot.

Secondly, must maintain vigilance at our borders. To date, to our knowledge about 150 United States persons have traveled to Syria or Iraq to fight along side ISIL, the new surf front and the like. There are known instances of a U.S. persons attempting to return from the region after participating in that conflict.

The more immediate threat, of course, is the thousands of individuals from our allied Nations in Europe, Northern Africa, and Middle East who have traveled to Syria undetected, gained terrorist training or military experience, that may now seek to travel. This is not an idle concern. The national contraries and system estimates that 20,000 individuals from 90 countries have traveled to fight in Syria.

Mr. Chairman, I have introduced H.R. 48, the ''No Fly for Foreign Fighters Act'' which I ask unanimous consent to enter into the record?

Mr. SENSENBRENNER. Without objection.

[The information referred to follows:]

114TH CONGRESS
1ST SESSION

H. R. 48

To require a review of the completeness of the Terrorist Screening Database (TSDB) maintained by the Federal Bureau of Investigation and the derivative terrorist watchlist utilized by the Transportation Security Administration, and for other purposes.

IN THE HOUSE OF REPRESENTATIVES

JANUARY 6, 2015

Ms. JACKSON LEE introduced the following bill; which was referred to the Committee on the Judiciary

---

A BILL

To require a review of the completeness of the Terrorist Screening Database (TSDB) maintained by the Federal Bureau of Investigation and the derivative terrorist watchlist utilized by the Transportation Security Administration, and for other purposes.

1   *Be it enacted by the Senate and House of Representa-*

2 *tives of the United States of America in Congress assembled,*

3 **SECTION 1. SHORT TITLE.**

4   This Act may be cited as the "No Fly for Foreign

5 Fighters Act".

SEC. 2. REVIEW OF THE COMPLETENESS OF THE TER-RORIST SCREENING DATABASE (TSDB) MAIN-TAINED BY THE FEDERAL BUREAU OF INVES-TIGATION AND THE DERIVATIVE TERRORIST WATCHLIST UTILIZED BY THE TRANSPOR-TATION SECURITY ADMINISTRATION.

(a) IN GENERAL.—Not later than 90 days after the date of the enactment of this Act, the Attorney General, acting through the Director of the Terrorist Screening Center, shall complete a review, in coordination with appropriate representatives from the Department of Homeland Security and all other relevant Federal agencies, of the completeness of the Terrorist Screening Database (TSDB) and the terrorist watchlist utilized by the Administrator of the Transportation Security Administration to determine if an individual who may seek to board a United States-bound flight or a domestic flight and who poses a threat to aviation or national security or a threat of terrorism and who is known or suspected of being a member of a foreign terrorist organization is included in such Database and on such watchlist.

(b) REPORT.—Not later than ten days after the completion of the review under subsection (a), the Director of the Terrorist Screening Center shall submit to the Committee on Homeland Security of the House of Representatives and the Committee on Homeland Security and Gov-

3

1 ernmental Affairs of the Senate a report on the findings

2 of such review.

○

Ms. JACKSON LEE. Which would require the government to review both terrorist screening database and the terrorist watch list for a complete list with respect to any of these foreign fighters and to report back to Congress with the results within 90 days.

Finally, we must fully fund, Mr. Chairman, the Department of Homeland Security without delay. The Islamic State is our focus today but is only one threat in an increasing complex landscape.

I would hope that we would again, as I know that the Chairman and myself have worked together with Members of the Judiciary Committee, that we enter into an effort to protect national security over political security. And I say that to reinforce the final words I want to offer of the Honorable Susan E. Spaulding who is the Under Secretary of National Protection and Programs Director of the U.S. Department of Homeland Security. Just her words in terms of the whole combination of threat and cybersecurity threats. ''As a nation, we are faced with pervasive cyber threats. Malicious actors, including those at nation-state level, are motivated by a variety of reasons that include espionage, political and ideological beliefs, and financial gain. Increasingly, state, local, tribal, and territorial networks are experiencing cyber activity of a sophistication level similar to that seen on Federal networks and has probably not been seen before.''

This hearing is a vital hearing because it squarely places us in the role of fighting terrorism. And I thank the Chairman very much and I thank the witnesses for their presence here today.

I yield back, Mr. Chairman.

Mr. SENSENBRENNER. Does the gentlewoman wish to include the statement that she just referred to in the record?

Ms. JACKSON LEE. I will ask unanimous consent, Mr. Chairman.

Mr. SENSENBRENNER. Without objection.

[The information referred to follows:]

Statement for the Record

The Honorable Suzanne E. Spaulding
Under Secretary, National Protection and Programs Directorate

Dr. Phyllis Schneck
Deputy Under Secretary, Cybersecurity and Communications

U.S. Department of Homeland Security

Before the
United States House of Representatives
Committee on Homeland Security

Regarding

Examining the President's Cybersecurity Information Sharing Proposal

February 25, 2015

Introduction

Chairman McCaul, Ranking Member Thompson, and distinguished Members of the Committee, we are pleased to appear today to discuss the President's cybersecurity legislative proposal on information sharing.

In our testimony today, we will highlight the Department of Homeland Security (DHS) National Protection and Programs Directorate cybersecurity role and capabilities, and describe how the President's legislative proposal to facilitate cyber threat indicator information sharing will further our national security, with DHS's National Cybersecurity and Communications Integration Center (NCCIC) as the coordination center to receive and disclose cyber threat indicators to Federal and Non-Federal entities.

The Ongoing Cyber Threat and the DHS Cybersecurity Role

As a nation, we are faced with pervasive cyber threats. Malicious actors, including those at nation-state level, are motivated by a variety of reasons that include espionage, political and ideological beliefs, and financial gain. Increasingly, State, Local, Tribal and Territorial (SLTT) networks are experiencing cyber activity of a sophistication level similar to that seen on Federal networks.

To achieve our cybersecurity mission, the National Protection and Programs Directorate focuses on helping our partners understand and manage cyber risk, reduce the frequency and impact of cyber incidents, and build partner capacity. We share timely and accurate information and analysis to enable private and public sector partners to protect themselves. We provide on-site assistance to Federal agencies and critical infrastructure entities impacted by a significant cybersecurity incident. We provide technology and services to detect and block cyber threats from impacting Federal civilian networks. We enable Federal agencies to more readily identify network security issues and take prioritized action. We enable commercial cybersecurity companies to use classified information so they can better protect their private sector customers. We perform comprehensive consequence analyses that assess cross-sector interdependencies and cascading effects, including the potential for kinetic harm that includes loss of life, and we maintain a trusted environment for private sector partners to share information and collaborate on cybersecurity threats and trends.

DHS's National Cybersecurity and Communications Integration Center

The NCCIC serves as a 24x7 centralized location for the coordination and integration of cyber situational awareness and incident management. NCCIC partners include all Federal departments and agencies; state, local, tribal, and territorial governments; the private sector; and international entities. The NCCIC continues to explore opportunities to expand its liaison capacity from other agencies and the private sector. The NCCIC provides its partners with enhanced situational awareness of cybersecurity and communications incidents and risks, and provides timely information to manage vulnerabilities, threats, and incidents. In 2014, the NCCIC received over 97,000 incident reports, and issued nearly 12,000 actionable cyber-alerts or warnings. NCCIC teams also detected over 64,000 significant vulnerabilities on federal and non-federal systems and directly responded to 115 significant cyber incidents.

The NCCIC actively shares cyber threat indicators to and from multiple sources including private sector partners, the Intelligence Community, Federal Departments and Agencies, law enforcement, State, Local, Tribal and Territorial governments, and international governments. This sharing, which has been taking place for many years, takes many forms including person-to-person interactions on the NCCIC floor, manual exchange of information via e-mail and secure web portals, and more recently via automated, machine-to-machine exchanges in STIX and TAXII protocols. While all of these sharing methods have value, the cybersecurity community has recognized the strategic importance of migrating cyber threat indicator sharing to more automated mechanisms when and where appropriate.

Cybersecurity Legislation

Last year, Congress acted in a bipartisan manner to pass critical cybersecurity legislation that enhanced the ability of the Department of Homeland Security to work with the private sector and other Federal civilian departments in each of their own cybersecurity activities, and enhanced the Department's cyber workforce authorities. Enactment of these bills represents a significant moment for the Department's cybersecurity mission, and this Committee in particular undertook significant efforts to bring the bills to passage. We are thankful for your support and we are deploying those additional authorities with clarity of mission.

Additional legislation is needed. We must take additional steps to ensure that DHS is able to rapidly and efficiently deploy new protective technologies across Federal civilian agency information systems. In addition, carefully updating laws to facilitate cybersecurity information sharing within the private sector and between the private and government sectors is also essential to improving the Nation's cybersecurity. While many companies currently share cybersecurity threat information under existing laws, there is a heightening need to increase the volume and speed of information shared without sacrificing the trust of the American people or the protection of privacy, confidentiality, civil rights, or civil liberties. It is essential to ensure that cyber threat information can be shared quickly among trusted partners, including with law enforcement, so that network owners and operators can take necessary steps to block threats and avoid damage.

The NCCIC plays a critical role in the President's recent legislative proposal because its core mission – as articulated in the National Cybersecurity Protection Act, developed by this Committee and unanimously-passed by the House in December – is to coordinate and serve as an interface for cybersecurity information across the government and private sector.

The Administration's Information Sharing Proposal for Cyber Threat Indicators

Building on the bipartisan cybersecurity legislation enacted last Congress, President Obama visited the NCCIC on January 13, 2015, to announce a proposal for additional legislation to improve cybersecurity information sharing. The President noted, "Much of our critical infrastructure runs on networks connected to the Internet....[a]nd most of this infrastructure is owned and operated by the private sector. So neither government nor the private sector can defend the nation alone. It's going to have to be a shared mission – government and industry working hand in hand, as partners." This partnership entails sharing cyber threat indicators to better enable government agencies and the private sector to protect themselves.

Information sharing, especially of these technical "threat indicators" that can be used to identify and block malicious activity, is the lifeblood of effective cyber defense and response. Pulling together this information allows defenders to identify anomalies or patterns and recognize dangerous activity before it can do significant damage. The goal of the President's proposal is to increase the sharing of this type of information, as quickly as possible, with appropriate protection for privacy and of sensitive information and systems.

Among other things, the Administration's proposal would reduce the risks for private entities to voluntarily share technical cyber threat indicators with each other and the NCCIC by providing protections against civil or criminal liability for such sharing. Equally important, the proposal narrowly defines the threat indicators that will be shared, requires that irrelevant identifying information be minimized from these indicators, and generally requires strong protections for the privacy and confidentiality of personal information. Finally, the proposal calls for the creation of Information Sharing and Analysis Organizations (ISAOs). ISAOs would be information sharing organizations that would help speed information sharing within the private sector and between the private sector and government.

Our goal is to expand information sharing within the private sector, and to build on the existing relationships, processes and programs of the NCCIC to enhance cooperation between the government and private sector. The proposal will help us improve the methods that the NCCIC already uses to share cyber threat indicators, and leverage automation to achieve scalability wherever possible. We look to evolve and expand indicator sharing at the NCCIC from human exchanges, portals, and written reports to automated machine-to-machine communications. Our vision is that this may reduce the time to receive and act on indicators from hours to milliseconds, create consistency in information provided to interagency partners, law enforcement, and the private sector, and free analysts to focus on the threats that require human analysis while expediting detection and blocking of new threats.

NCCIC as the Coordination Center

Cyber threat indicators, which allow government agencies and the private sector to better protect themselves, come from a variety of sources, including: government agencies, private companies, international partners, and ISAOs. Given the variety of formats used – and information that is included – when sharing such information, the government must have a central clearinghouse to ensure that privacy and confidentiality protections are consistently applied and that the right information reaches the right government and private sector entities.

DHS is a leader within the government when it comes to the development and operational implementation of privacy, confidentiality, and civil liberties policies. DHS was the first agency to have statutorily established Officers for Privacy and for Civil Rights and Civil Liberties. From its creation, DHS has built both privacy and civil liberties protections into all of its programs and has dedicated, on-site privacy professionals committed to ensuring that its cyber mission is carried out in a way consistent with our Nation's values. Through statutory protections like Protected Critical Infrastructure Information (PCII), DHS will continue to anonymize the identity of submitters and other proprietary and sensitive information in threat indicator submissions. Moreover, the President's proposal calls for DHS to build upon its existing privacy, confidentiality, and civil liberty procedures by working with the

Attorney General to develop new procedures to appropriately limit Government receipt, use, and retention of threat indicators. Establishing the NCCIC as the primary entry way for cyber threat indicators from the private sector will ensure uniform application of these important privacy and confidentiality protections, while still allowing cyber threat indictors to be shared with law enforcement for the specific purposes identified in the legislation.

NCCIC sits at the intersection of cyber communities, with representatives from the private sector and other government entities physically present on the NCCIC floor and connected virtually. This diverse participation in the NCCIC was cemented by section 226(d) of the Homeland Security Act as added by the National Cybersecurity Protection Act. NCCIC's core mission is to enable better network defense by assessing and appropriately sharing information on the risks to America's critical cyber systems and how to reduce them.

Building Capacity to Accelerate Automated Sharing of Cyber Threat Indicators

The Administration's proposal directs DHS to automate and share information in as close to real-time as practicable with relevant federal agencies, including law enforcement entities, and with ISAOs. For the past three years, DHS has led the development in collaboration with the private sector of specifications – known as STIX and TAXII – which standardize the representation and exchange of cyber threat information, including actionable cyber threat indicators. STIX, the Structured Threat Information eXpression, is a standardized format for the representation and exchange of cyber threat information, including indicators. TAXII, the Trusted Automated eXchange of Indicator Information, is a standardized protocol for discovering and exchanging cyber threat information in STIX. The interagency Enhance Shared Situational Awareness initiative has already chosen STIX as the basis for sharing cyber threat indicators between the Federal cyber centers, ensuring interoperability between these key sources of information.

Through collaboration between DHS and the private sector, there is a solid and rapidly growing base of commercial offerings supporting STIX and sharing indicators via the TAXII, including platforms, network protection appliances and endpoint security tools. While the NCCIC has in-house systems and tools to assist analysts in generating STIX indicators, those indicators are currently analyzed and filtered by human analysts and shared back out with the private sector and Federal partners through manual methods such as e-mail and secure portals. In 2014, the NCCIC began a limited pilot with several organizations to test automated delivery of STIX indicators via TAXII.

To inform our plan for achieving automated cyber threat indicator information sharing, DHS created a working group between a range of DHS offices and the FBI, a critical stakeholder in the NCCIC. We also included experts from our Privacy, Civil Rights and Civil Liberties, and Science and Technology offices, among others, to ensure that our architecture is based on best-in-class technology and is consistent with our values and our respect for Americans' privacy and civil liberties.

Implementation will proceed through four major phases: (1) an initial operating capability phase in which we will deploy a TAXII system that can disseminate STIX cyber threat indicators with increased automation capability, enabling the use of human analysis for the most complex problems and egregious threats; (2) an expanded automation phase in which we will develop and deploy DHS infrastructure that can receive, filter, and analyze cyber threat indicators-- during this phase, we will promulgate guidance for private sector companies to minimize, redact and tag their data prior to submission to NCCIC, and will complete a Privacy Impact Assessment; (3) a final operating capability phase in which we will fully automate DHS processes to receive and appropriately disseminate cyber threat indicators in a machine-readable format and finalize policies for filtering, receipt, retention, use, and sharing, including regular compliance reviews; and (4) a scaled services capability phase, during which DHS will work to enable agencies that lack sufficient cybersecurity resources or expertise to receive and share cyber threat indicators with the NCCIC in near-real-time by providing a turnkey technical solution to "plug in" to the NCCIC.

DHS Shares Information Widely with Federal Agencies and the Private Sector

Currently, DHS shares information with Federal Agencies and the private sector. DHS takes a customer-focused approach to information sharing, and different types of information require differing response times and dissemination protocols. DHS provides information to detect and block cybersecurity attacks on Federal civilian agencies and shares information to help critical infrastructure entities in their own protection; provides information to commercial cybersecurity companies so they can better protect their customers through the Enhanced Cybersecurity Services program, or ECS; and maintains a trusted information sharing environment for private sector partners to share information and collaborate on cybersecurity threats and trends via a program known as the Cyber Information Sharing and Collaboration Program, or CISCP. This trust derives in large part from our emphasis on privacy, confidentiality, civil rights, and civil liberties across all information sharing programs, including special care to safeguard personally identifiable information.

DHS also directly supports Federal civilian departments and agencies in developing capabilities that will improve their own cybersecurity posture. Through the Continuous Diagnostics and Mitigation (CDM) program, DHS enables Federal agencies to more readily identify network security issues, including unauthorized and unmanaged hardware and software; known vulnerabilities; weak configuration settings; and potential insider attacks. Agencies can then prioritize mitigation of these issues based upon potential consequences or likelihood of exploitation by adversaries. The CDM program provides diagnostic sensors, tools, and dashboards that provide situational awareness to individual agencies, and will provide DHS with summary data to understand relative and system risk across the Executive Branch. DHS is moving aggressively to implement CDM across all Federal civilian agencies, and Memoranda of Agreement with the CDM program encompass over 97 percent of all Federal civilian personnel.

While CDM will identify vulnerabilities and systemic risks within agency networks, the National Cybersecurity Protection System, also known as EINSTEIN, detects and blocks threats at the perimeter of those networks or at an agencies' Internet Service Provider. EINSTEIN is an integrated intrusion detection, analysis, information sharing, and intrusion-prevention system. The most recent iteration, Einstein 3 Accelerated (E3a), supplements EINSTEIN 2 by adding additional intrusion prevention capabilities and enabling Internet Service Providers (ISPs), under the direction of DHS, to detect and block known or suspected cyber threats using indicators.

Conclusion

We are working together to find new and better ways to share accurate, timely data in a manner consistent with fundamental American values of privacy, confidentiality, and civil rights. While securing cyberspace has been identified as a core DHS mission since the 2010 Quadrennial Homeland Security Review, the Department's view of cybersecurity has evolved to include a more holistic emphasis on critical infrastructure which takes into account the convergence of cyber and physical risk.

Today our adversaries exploit a fundamental asymmetry in our network infrastructure: while nearly all of our systems and networks are globally interconnected, our defensive capabilities are not. This gives the attackers a compelling advantage as they can find and exploit the weak links in our systems from anywhere around the world – at machine speed. By sharing cyber threat indicators in near real-time, we reduce that asymmetry.

As our defensive cybersecurity capabilities become more interconnected, we greatly reduce the likelihood that an adversary can re-use attack infrastructure, tools, tactics, techniques and procedures. In addition, we greatly reduce the time window in which new and novel attacks are effective because the ecosystem shares those indicators and develops a type of "herd immunity," improving defenses as indicators are shared and events are correlated in near-real-time. These two factors do not eliminate all cyber threats, but they hold the promise of significantly increasing the time and resources (both technical and human) that attackers must expend to achieve their goals. Moreover, the STIX data format and the TAXII transport method are increasingly compatible with commonly used commercial information technology (IT) products. This means more entities are able to send indicators automatically to the NCCIC, creating an ecosystem of indicators which will in turn provide greater context to malicious cyber activity and rapidly increase situational awareness per Executive Order 13636, *Improving Critical Infrastructure Cybersecurity* and Executive Order 13691, signed February 13, 2015, *Promoting Private Sector Cybersecurity Information Sharing.*

DHS will continue to serve as one of the government's primary resources for information sharing and collaborative analysis, at machine-speed wherever possible, of global cyber risks, trends, and incidents. Through our leadership role in protecting civilian government systems and helping the private sector protect itself, DHS can correlate data from diverse sources, in an anonymized and secure manner, to maximize insights and inform effective risk mitigation.

DHS provides the foundation of the U.S. government's approach to securing and ensuring the resilience of civilian critical infrastructure and essential services. We look forward to continuing the conversation and supporting the American goals of peace and stability; in these endeavors, we rely upon your continued support.

Thank you for the opportunity to testify, and we look forward to any questions you may have.

Ms. Jackson Lee. Thank you.

Mr. Sensenbrenner. The Chair recognizes the Chair of the full Committee, gentleman from Virginia, Mr. Goodlatte.

Mr. Goodlatte. Thank you, Chairman Sensenbrenner.

With increasing regularity, Americans are being witnessed to the depravity of terrorists claiming the mantle of the Islamic State of Iraq and the Levant, or ISIL. Relatively unknown to many in America just a few years ago, ISIL relishes in their own barbarity with videos depicting shootings, beheadings, and the burning alive of unarmed prisoners.

Recently, ISIL claimed to mark the occasion of conquering a small town in western Iraq by burning 45 of its inhabitants at the stake. The group's history gives us little reason to dismiss this as hyperbole. And ISIL's savagery is limited no more by geography than by human decency. Earlier this month in Libya, hundreds of miles from the group's claimed territory, ISIL terrorists rounded up and videotaped themselves decapitating 21 Egyptian Christians who refused to renounce Christ and accept ISIL as their new masters.

Americans are not mere observers of ISIL's atrocities. Our people and our homeland are intimate parts of ISIL's plans. The organization's leadership had attacks on America and the rest of the West. They have solicited young people to renounce their lives and join them in their perverted war. Unfortunately, even deep in the American heartland, these calls have found some receptive ears.

Speaking in Jackson, Mississippi earlier this month, FBI Director James Comey emphasized that city is not beyond ISIL's reach. He urged law enforcement and American citizens everywhere to be vigilant and not dismiss the domestic threat from extremism. Just yesterday, Director Comey disclosed that the Bureau is investigating suspected supporters of ISIL in every U.S. state.

Director Comey's concerns are borne out by the facts. The last several years have seen three distinct threats to the homeland from Levantine terrorism. The first is the recruitment of young Americans into the ISIL fold. In addition to thousands of Europeans, over 150 Americans have been discovered joining in the fighting in the Middle East or attempting to do so.

Those who have taken up the ISIL banner fit no social, ethnic, or even gender profile. Douglas McAuthur McCain grew up in Chicago and Minneapolis with a close-knit family. He was a popular joker in high school and a devoted fan of the Chicago Bulls. Last summer, a tattoo of his was used to confirm him as the first American to be killed fighting for the terrorists in Syria.

Young women are also being recruited, lured to leave their families and become Jihad wives of ISIL fighters. Shannon Conley, a teenager from Arvada, Colorado was arrested at Denver International Airport last April in route to her arranged marriage with a 32-year old Tunisian Jihadi. She had changed her Facebook status to ''Slave of Allah'' and told FBI agents she looked forward to using the skills she learned in the U.S. Army Explorers program to nurse wounded ISIL fighters.

If and when these Americans choose to return to the United States from the battlefields of a brutal civil war, it will be difficult to stop them reentering. It will be even more difficult to know what they are capable of. We know, for example, that last month's Charlie Hebdo shooters had traveled to the Middle East and received training from Jihadi groups.

The second threat, perhaps even more dangerous, requires no travel beyond the nearest computer. The Western World has been plagued by a rash of attacks by self-radicalized lone-wolf terrorists who have claimed allegiance to ISIL. Last year, Canada suffered two serious terrorist attacks by ISIL adherents who had never gotten closer to the group than their Internet message boards. One man drove his car into a group of Canadian Forces soldiers; the other murdered a soldier before attempting to storm the Canadian Parliament.

In Australia, a man took 18 people hostage at a chocolate shop, killing two of them. In Belgium, a man shot dead four people at a Jewish Museum. All of these terrorist committed their attacks under the banner of ISIL.

Finally, we must not forget that the core group of ISIL, half a world away, plots to attack us directly here in the homeland. This last month, ISIL's central command reiterated their intention to attack American policemen, soldiers, and members of our intelligence community.

I look forward to hearing from our witnesses today about these threats, how they are evolving domestically, and the challenges our intelligence and law enforcement officials face in thwarting these violent terrorist and those who pledge allegiance to them here in our homeland. I also hope to hear how Congress and this Committee can best ensure that our country is prepared to stop these threats.

Thank you, Mr. Chairman.

Mr. SENSENBRENNER. Time of the gentleman has expired.

The Chair now recognizes for his opening statement, the Ranking Member and Chairman emeritus of the full Committee, the gentleman from Michigan, Mr. Conyers.

Mr. CONYERS. Thank you, Chairman Sensenbrenner. And to all of my colleagues here, particularly those who have made opening statements.

I am deeply concerned about the rise of the Islamic State in Iraq and the Levant, ISIL. It is a grave regional threat operating from Anbar province and Western Iraq, it seized territory from Baghdad to Aleppo, and continues to press north into Kurdish territory. In more familiar terms, ISIL now controls an area larger than the United Kingdom.

Along the way, it has directed horrific violence at thousands of civilians, particularly ethnic and religious minorities, and ISIL has also executed hostages including four United States citizens in barbaric and public fashion. So we should not underestimate ISIL's murderous intent nor its ability to inspire others to do us harm. But we've learned much from the past decade of fighting radical extremists and it seems important today to apply some of those lessons in our discussion.

The first and most simple lesson is don't panic. As of this morning, the Department of Homeland Security is unaware of any specific credible threat to the United States homeland from ISIL. The National Counterterrorism Center confirms that assessment noting further that any threat to the U.S. homeland from these types of extremists is likely to be limited in scope and in scale. I do not suggest that we in any way ignore ISIL or the suffering it has caused. No way. But I do point out only that the group's ability to strike directly at the United States appears to be limited and that our reaction to the home front should be measured and appropriate.

The rise of the Islamic State is not an excuse for domestic law enforcement to stigmatize American Muslims. It does not legitimatize tactics that have isolated and alienated the communities whose help we need most. Nor does the threat of ISIL justify the government's continued use of Section 215 of the U.S.A. Patriot Act to conduct mass surveillance on law-abiding citizens. The mass telephone metadata program has never disrupted a terrorist plot, does not extend to the new media formats favored by ISIL, and must be brought to an end without delay.

We have better tools at our disposal which leads me to this consideration: Our best hope for countering the threat of radicalization at home is community engagement at the local level. We haven't evidence of a direct threat from ISIL on the U.S. homeland but as my colleagues have noted the group has an aggressive social medial presence. Their propaganda targets the most isolated elements of our society. We know what works to counter this messaging. Local, state, and Federal law enforcement must build partnerships with teachers, clergy, and other community leaders. These efforts must clearly preserve religious exercise and freedom of expression.

Once we have established trust and open lines of communication between police and the communities most at risk for radicalization, we win on two fronts. We are better able to identify potential threats before they go dangerous and community leaders have enlisted a powerful partner in countering the twisted rhetoric of ISIL and others like it.

I believe the witnesses here today will testify to the effectiveness of this basic approach and I look forward to further discussion with them on the matter. And perhaps most pressing at this late hour, we must fully fund the Department of Homeland Security.

Mr. Chairman, I believe it comes down to a question of priorities. We must preserve the capability to track foreign fighters before they attempt to enter the United States. We must keep the United States Air Marshalls in the sky and we must continue to coordinate with our agents on the front lines of homeland security, the transportation Safety Administration, the United States Customs and Border Patrol and our own partners in state, local and tribal law enforcement.

Some of these functions may continue in the event of a shutdown but many will not. Most of the department's leadership team will be furloughed. Federal support to state and local initiatives will terminate, none of the officers who must show up to work will necessarily be paid. And so, my colleagues, there was a time when I believed that we could find common ground on a comprehensive immigration reform. I still believe that. If Speaker Boehner would allow the measure to come to the floor, the bill that has sat on his desk for more than 500 days would receive majority support in the House. But even if we must disagree for now on the urgency of immigration reform, surely we can agree that we must not compromise our national security in a futile effort to score political points against the president.

Whatever you think of the underlying policy, a decision to defund the Department of Homeland Security simply will not result in the president's reversing his actions on immigration.

I agree with you, Mr. Chairman, that the threat posed by ISIL to the homeland is real. I hope that our conversation today will convince my colleagues to prioritize our security over an unrelated political spat and fully fund DHS, Department of Homeland Security, without delay.

I too join in welcoming our witnesses. I thank the Chairman and yield back.

Mr. SENSENBRENNER. The gentleman's time has expired long ago.

Without objection, other Member's opening statements will be made apart of the record.

Today we have a very distinguished panel of witnesses. I will begin by swearing in our witnesses before introducing them.

If you would please rise.

Do you solemnly swear that the testimony that you are about give to this Committee will be the truth, the whole truth, and nothing but the truth so help you God?

Let the record show that all of the witnesses have answered in the affirmative.

Charlotte Police Chief, Rodney Monroe, is unable to be here today due to the weather and his written testimony will be entered into the record without objection.

[The prepared statement of Mr. Monroe follows:]

TESTIMONY OF

RODNEY MONROE, CHIEF OF POLICE

ON BEHALF OF
CHARLOTTE MECKLENBURG POLICE DEPARTMENT

AND

MAJOR CITIES CHIEFS ASSOCIATION

BEFORE THE

JUDICIARY COMMITTEE

SUB COMMITTEE ON CRIME, TERRORISM, HOMELAND SECURITY, AND
INVESTIGATIONS

UNITED STATES HOUSE OF REPRESENTATIVES

"State and Local Approaches to Countering Violent Extremism"

February 26, 2015

Chairman Sensenbrenner, we are grateful for this opportunity to address a growing threat across our Nation. Ranking member Lee, let me thank you for appearing at our recent meeting in Washington and I bring regards from my colleague and your own Chief in Houston.

Chairman Goodlatte, we thank you for attending this meeting of your Subcommittee, as this demonstrates your commitment and deep concern. Ranking Member Conyers and distinguished Members, today I speak for the Major Cities Chiefs of Police, representing the 67 largest cities in the Nation, as well as my own department and city. Sheriff Stanek and I appear before you to represent every major urban area, and the majority of the American population. Preventing terrorism and protecting the public are our top priorities, and we thank you today on behalf of the public we are sworn to protect.

I am the Chief of the Charlotte-Mecklenburg Police Department, with nearly 2,000 officers and jurisdiction over the largest city in North Carolina. Our county is home to nearly a million citizens and the Nation's second largest financial center. Our community includes a multitude of Fortune 500 companies, cultural landmarks and the headquarters or major hub for extensive critical infrastructure. Terrorism is a real threat that we face every day – both the Sheriff and I face threats of attack at public shopping malls in our communities.

Domestic terrorism is prevalent. It's not something that is simply going to disappear. To truly eradicate extremism in the United States and abroad, well thought out actions and established precautionary measures must be taken. As the number and variety of terrorism incidents and cases shows, violent extremism can be found everywhere – not only in cities like New York, Chicago or Los Angeles. Also where you may not expect to find it, in communities like my own Charlotte or as my colleague describes today, Minneapolis.

We have a responsibility to our Nation's people to keep them safe and to our children so that they can grow up in a country where they don't live in constant fear of violent extremism. Countering Violent Extremism, or CVE, involves diligence in making sure we are aware of those who have been radicalized and what their potential is to carry out threats.

This threat has evolved from the central core of Al Qaida, to diverse 'Lone Wolf' style threats, and now to the threat of foreign fighters travelling to and from the United States with military style training. These fighters, as American citizens, permanent residents, or the citizens of countries that are traditionally considered safe travelers pose a highly dangerous threat to our Nation. They fit no stereotype, they have the freedom of movement to visit anywhere, and they possess battle hardened training that makes them the ideal candidate to commit a terrorist act on the Homeland. North Carolina has not been immune.

Home-grown Terrorists

In our state, one of the more recent examples of domestic terrorism involved Donald Morgan of Salisbury, North Carolina. Morgan didn't favor well in the army or in his law enforcement career due to bad life decisions. He eventually converted to Islam, became radical, and started posting messages on social media outlets in support of terrorism. Eventually he tried to join an extremist group before being arrested for gun trafficking.

No one can really say what will lead someone to turn his or her back on our country and pledge allegiance to violent extremism. Therefore, it is our job as law enforcement professionals to do everything in our power to capture self-radicalized individuals on the front end before it is too late.

Foreign Ties to the Homeland

In 2014, two North Carolina extremists were Akba Jordan and Basit Sheikh. Jordan, 22, of Raleigh, pleaded guilty to conspiracy to provide material support to terrorists. Jordan and co-defendant Avin Marsalis Brown, 21, also of Raleigh, were arrested on March 19, 2014, and charged initially in a criminal complaint. On April 1, 2014, a federal grand jury returned an indictment charging Jordan and Brown with conspiring to provide material support to terrorists.

On March 19, 2014, Brown was arrested at Raleigh Durham International Airport prior to boarding a flight with a final destination in Turkey. Brown intended to travel from Turkey into Syria. Once overseas, he was to meet with a member of ISIS whom he had befriended online. Once established, and after Jordan had obtained his own passport and enough funds to purchase a ticket, Brown could then assist Jordan in entering Syria from Turkey to additionally join Brown.

Foreign Fighters in the Homeland

Another example of terrorism here at home involved Basit Javed Sheikh. On November 5, 2013, a federal grand jury in Raleigh returned an indictment charging Sheikh with attempting to provide material support and resources to a foreign terrorist organization.

The indictment charges that Sheikh attempted to provide material support and resources to Jabhat al-Nusrah which the United States Secretary of State has identified as an alias name for al Qaeda in Iraq, a designated Foreign Terrorist Organization. The affidavit describes multiple Facebook postings by Sheikh since April, 2013, expressing support Nusrah which has claimed responsibility for nearly 600 attacks in Syria that have killed numerous innocent civilians. Sheikh reached out to the covert FBI employee and expressed his desire to travel to Syria in order to "help the mujahedeen...in any way I can." When asked how he wanted to help, Sheikh responded "logistics, media, fight too, God willing."

Despite the FBI covert employee stating to Sheikh that fighting was not for everyone, Sheikh informed the FBI covert employee that he was "serious" and that he was ready to be a martyr. On November 2, 2013, Sheikh traveled to Raleigh-Durham Airport, and was arrested prior to boarding his flight.

Role of the Internet

One of our early cases remains an example to this day. Charlotte resident Samir Khan is an illustration of the terrorist threat in our homeland, and the role of the internet. While the case of Mr. Khan predates the formation of ISIL, Mr. Khan's story shows how far back the tentacles of racialization may reach. Mr. Khan travelled to Yemen after living in Charlotte and founded AQAP's *Inspire Magazine*. While Samir Khan was killed several years ago, his magazine continues to be published to this day with information for domestically based extremists to execute attacks. Widely read and very professional in appearance, his internet-based magazine has included information on how to build specialty bombs and has targeted high profile venues.

We are not going to win this fight with traditional methods and each of the cases I have cited are examples of radicalization and training via the internet. Law enforcement agencies need tech savvy staff who can quickly digest information in real time. Additionally, they need to help us in getting ahead of ever evolving technology while at the same time assist us in pushing out counter messages of extremism.

The obvious pattern with the referenced cases is use of the internet to become a self-radical and a clear desire to travel abroad in support of international terrorism. Radicals have a common thread of wanting a cause to believe in and a sense of belonging to a larger, well established entity.

Joint Terrorism Task Force (JTTF)

Countering violent extremism requires that we execute strategies which involve an unwavering trust among agencies involved in the fight. The Charlotte-Mecklenburg Police Department (CMPD) has a strong relationship with our agency partners in sharing information on CVE. Each of the cases I have noted were joint operations that included Federal, State and local agencies. Every one of them was truly a team effort.

CMPD is fortunate to work with a knowledgeable group of men and women who represent 44 local, state and Federal agencies on the Charlotte Joint Terrorism Task Force (JTTF). This is a phenomenal collaboration with Federal, state, and local partners. No one agency can do it alone.

Charlotte JTTF has been extremely successful with CVE. One of the most effective tools we have for thwarting plots is sharing of information. The benefit of being a part of JTTF is that it allows for the free flow of information on potential threats between agency partners.

As chief, my role on JTTF is to ensure that CMDP shares its resources in helping to identify potential threats. Our task force members have been able to leverage their positions in helping us identify homegrown threats.

Community Resolve

While JTTF efforts have been successful, we know it doesn't stop there. Domestic terrorists aren't necessarily out in the open. They hide behind cyber walls while spreading their messages of destruction and terror. The face of domestic extremists varies as there is a wide range of economical, geographical and age factors. They all look different. The only commonality is the use the internet to spread violent extremism. Our greatest protection for the public is the public itself. Local police and sheriffs are engaged with their communities to detect and prevent violent extremism at the most early stages of radicalization, before it becomes criminal and becomes another case at the JTTF. When we build relationships of trust with the community, we learn about persons who may pose a threat to public safety before it is too late. Chiefs and Sheriffs have built strong partnerships with the public we serve - to stop extremism in all forms

Criminal Intelligence Enterprise

Charlotte stands with our sister metropolitan areas in addressing this pervasive threat. As a member of the Major Cities Chiefs, we are participating in the Criminal Intelligence Enterprise (CIE) which is recognized in the 2015 Appropriations Bill. CIE is a local threat identification and assessment process that helps police agencies determine their priority criminal threats. Standardized protocols are used by criminal intelligence units and fusion centers to determine and substantiate their criminal threats and their intelligence collection needs. This program is particularly salient to identifying and preventing violent extremism

Fusion Centers and DHS

Through funding provided by a partnership with the Department of Homeland Security, Chiefs and Sheriffs of this Nation are better enabled to counter the extremist threat and better able to coordinate criminal intelligence matters. This could not happen without DHS and regional fusion centers. We are thankful to Congress for supporting this program via the appropriations process and to the Department of Homeland Security for providing the portal platform from which this program will expand. Major Cities Chiefs Association maintains a Homeland Security Committee that coordinates our efforts to disseminate best practices, coordinate police operations, interaction with our Federal partners and to address new and rising concerns such as ISIL. We believe strongly that fusion centers and DHS must be equal partners in all aspects of our work. Without them we do not have a comprehensive strategy.

Stronger Information Sharing

Following the Boston Marathon bombings, the House looked into information sharing at JTTFs. Learning lessons from gaps in information sharing in Boston, Chiefs and Sheriffs have sought to build a stronger JTTF process. Major Cities Chiefs addressed a list of concerns with FBI Director Comey and we have engaged the FBI in an ongoing dialogue to strengthen information sharing. I am pleased to report to the Subcommittee that the FBI responded to our specific concerns with a directive to all field offices implementing critical policy changes. Speaking for Charlotte and my own region, I can assure members of the Subcommittee that information sharing has never been more effective. Is it always perfect? Of course not. But our teamwork is stronger than ever before. The cases I have cited today are examples of a law enforcement community that is resourceful and united in our commitment to protect the public.

The Way Forward

Terrorism is no longer something that we only hear about in other countries. It is here, right in our own backyards or even residing at our next door neighbor's house. Countering violent extremism is our most viable options to keeping our citizens and country safe from those who would see us suffer and die.

We must build upon increasing awareness, communication, and inter-agency cooperation in order to propel the CVE strategy to its highest potential. Then and only then will we be one step closer to erasing terrorism and achieving the ultimate dream of peace and a much safer world for the generations to come.

Chairman Sensenbrenner, Ranking Member Lee, and Distinguished Members of the Subcommittee - those of us on the front lines look to you for leadership and support. Local law enforcement is charged with the solemn duty to discover, disrupt and stop plots hatched within the U.S. Please know that my colleagues and I are committed to the goal shared by each of you – the prevention of all crimes, terrorist plots, and threats to the homeland including the interdiction of those who would bring us harm. We need your continued help to be successful, and I look forward to working with both the Subcommittee and the full Committee in the future.

Thank you and I look forward to your questions.

Mr. SENSENBRENNER. Michael B. Steinbach is the Assistant Director of the Counter Terrorism Division. Mr. Steinbach began at the FBI in the Chicago Division. He has served as head of the Violent Crimes Taskforce at the FBI's Washington Field Office, the Assistant Section Chief for the International Terrorism Operations Section of the Counterterrorism Division, and as Deputy Director for Law Enforcement Services at the CIES Counterterrorism Center. He was then appointed as Special Assistant to the Associate Deputy Director at FBI Headquarters. Mr. Steinbach has also served as the Special Agent-in-Charge of the FBI's Jacksonville Division and later as the Special Agent-in-Charge of the Miami Division.

Sorry you are coming to the snowy parts and you are at the end of your career.

Mr. Steinbach has earned a Bachelor's of Science Degree in aerospace engineering from the U.S. Naval Academy in 1988 after which he served as a Naval Aviator in the U.S. Navy.

Richard W. Stanek, who is familiar as I am with weather like this, is the Sheriff of Hennepin County, Minnesota. In this role he created a new crime fighting unit at the Sheriff's Office to serve law enforcement agencies and communities county-wide. Sheriff Stanek began his career at the Minneapolis Police Department, he rose through the ranks from patrol officer to commander of criminal investigations. While a police officer he was elected five times to the Minnesota legislature where he authored the State's DWI felony law. In 2003, the governor appointed him Commissioner of Public Safety and Director of Homeland Security for Minnesota. Sheriff Stanek earned a criminal justice degree from the University of Minnesota and a Master's Degree in public administration from Hamline University.

You are all familiar with the green, yellow, and red lights in front of you. I would ask that you limit your testimony to a 5-minute summary after which the Committee Members will ask questions under the 5-minute rule.

Mr. Steinbach, you are first.

TESTIMONY OF MICHAEL STEINBACH, ASSISTANT DIRECTOR, FEDERAL BUREAU OF INVESTIGATION

Mr. STEINBACH. Thank you, sir.

Good morning, Chairman Sensenbrenner, Ranking Member Lee, and Members of the Committee. It is also good to see Ranking Member Conyers present and I appreciate Chairman Goodlatte's opening remarks.

Thank you for the opportunity to appear before you today to discuss the dynamic threat of foreign fighters traveling in support of the Islamic State of Iraq and the Levant, commonly known as ISIL, and the continued threat to the United States posed by homegrown violent extremists. These threats remain one of the biggest priorities for the FBI, the intelligence community, and our foreign, state, and local partners. It is the blending of the homegrown violent extremism with the foreign fighter ideology which is today's latest adaptation of the threat. I am pleased to be here today with a strong state and local partner, Hennepin County Sheriff, Richard Stanek.

Conflicts in Syria and Iraq are currently the most attractive overseas threats for Western-based extremists who want to engage in violence. We estimate upwards of 150 Americans have traveled or attempted to travel to Syria. While this number is small in comparison to the number of European travelers, we must also consider the influence of groups like ISIL have on individuals located in the United States who are inspired to commit acts of violence. It is this influence which I refer to as the blended threat.

ISIL has proven ruthless in its violent campaign to rule and has become yet the latest terror group attracting like-minded Western extremists. Yet, from a homeland perspective, it is ISIL's widespread reach through the Internet and social media which is the most concerning as ISIL has proven dangerously competent like no other group before it at employing such tools for its nefarious strategy.

ISIL utilizes high-quality traditional media platforms as well as a multitude of most social media campaigns to propagate its extremist ideas. Like al-Qaeda and other foreign terrorist organizations, ISIL has effectively used the Internet to communicate, to both radicalize and recruit. Unlike other groups, ISIL has gone one step further and demonstrates an effectiveness to spot and assess potential recruits.

Social media, in particular, has provided ISIL with a technical platform for widespread recruitment, operational direction, and, consequently, has helped bridge the gap between foreign fighters and homegrown violent extremists.

As a communication tool, the Internet remains a critical node for terror groups to exploit. One recent example occurred just a few weeks ago. A group of five individuals was arrested for knowingly and willingly conspiring and attempting to provide material support and resources to a designated foreign terrorist organization active in Syria and Iraq. Much of their conspiracy occurred on the Internet.

Following on other group's doctrines, ISIL too has advocated for lone wolf attacks. Last month, ISIL released a video via social media reiterating the group's encouragement of lone offender attacks in Western countries, specifically advocating for attacks against soldiers and law enforcement and intelligence members. Several incidents have occurred in the United States and Europe over the past few months thato indicate this call-to-arms has resonated among ISIL supporters and sympathizers.

In one case, an Ohio-based man was arrested in January after he obtained a weapon and stated his intent to conduct an attack on the U.S. Capitol here in Washington, D.C. Using a Twitter account, the individual posted statements, videos, and other content indicating support for ISIL and he planned an attack based on his voiced support.

Likewise, recent events in Australia, Canada, France, and the U.K. reflect the power of this radicalized message and reemphasize our need to remain vigilant in the homeland since these small-scale attacks are just as feasible within the United States. We should also understand community and world events as viewed through the eyes of the committed individual may trigger action as we have seen with the highly publicized events of the attack on the military personnel at the Tomb of the Unknown Soldier in Canada and the hostage situation at the café? in Australia. These acts of terror will attract international attention and may inspire copycat attacks.

ISIL is not the only high profile terrorist organization of concern, however. Al-Qaeda in the Arabian Peninsula, or AQAP, poses an ongoing threat to the homeland and U.S. interests abroad. AQAP's online English magazine Inspire advocates for lone wolf attacks to conduct attacks against the homeland and Western targets by utilizing simple and inexpensive tactics and methods.

Lastly, social media has allowed groups such as ISIL to use the Internet even more effectively by spotting assessing potential recruits. With the widespread distribution of the social media, terrorists can identify sympathetic individuals of all ages in the United States. Spot, assess, recruit, and radicalize, either to travel or to conduct a homeland attack. The foreign terrorist now has direct access into the United States like never before.

As a result, it is imperative that the FBI and all law enforcement organizations understand the latest communication tools and are equipped to identify and prevent terror attacks in the homeland. We live in a technologically driven society and, just as private industry has adapted to these modern forms of communication, so too has the terrorists. Unfortunately, changing forms of communication on the Internet and through social media are quickly outpacing the laws and the technology designed to allow for lawful intercept of communication content.

This real and growing gap the FBI refers to as ''Going Dark'' cannot be ignored. We must continue to build partnerships and work with Internet providers and social media companies to ensure lawful, appropriate collection when possible. Most companies are not required by statute to develop lawful intercept capabilities for law enforcement. As a result, services are developed and deployed without any ability to lawfully intercept and collect.

The FBI, with our Federal, state, and local partners is utilizing all investigative techniques and methods to combat the threat radicalizing individuals may pose to the United States. In coordination with our domestic and foreign partners, we are rigorously collecting and analyzing intelligence information as it pertains to the ongoing threat posed by ISIL, AQAP, and other foreign terrorist organizations.

I will end my comments here and put the rest in the record.

[The prepared statement of Mr. Steinbach follows:]

 **Department of Justice**

STATEMENT OF

**MICHAEL STEINBACH
ASSISTANT DIRECTOR
FEDERAL BUREAU OF INVESTIGATION**

BEFORE THE

**COMMITTEE ON THE JUDICIARY
SUBCOMMITTEE ON CRIME, TERRORISM,
HOMELAND SECURITY, AND INVESTIGATIONS
UNITED STATES HOUSE OF REPRESENTATIVES**

ENTITLED

"ISLAMIC STATE & DOMESTIC TERRORISM"

PRESENTED

FEBRUARY 26, 2015

Statement of Michael Steinbach
Assistant Director
Federal Bureau of Investigation

Before the
Committee on the Judiciary
Subcommittee on Crime, Terrorism, Homeland Security, and Investigations
United States House of Representatives

At a Hearing Entitled
"Islamic State & Domestic Terrorism"
Presented
February 26, 2015

Good morning Chairman Sensenbrenner, Ranking Member Lee, and Members of the Committee. Thank you for the opportunity to appear before you today to discuss the dynamic threat posed by foreign fighters traveling in support of the Islamic State of Iraq and the Levant (ISIL) and the continued threat to the United States posed by homegrown violent extremists. These threats remain one of the biggest priorities for the Federal Bureau of Investigation (FBI), the Intelligence Community (IC), and our foreign, state and local partners. I am pleased to be here today with strong state and local partners - Charlotte, North Carolina Police Chief, Rodney Monroe and Hennepin County, Minneapolis, Minnesota Sheriff Richard Stanek.

As you know, the conflict in Syria and Iraq is currently the most attractive overseas theater for Western-based extremists who want to engage in violence. We estimate upwards of 150 Americans have traveled or attempted to travel to Syria to join extremist groups. While this number is small in comparison to the number of European travelers, we must also consider the influence groups like ISIL have on individuals located in the United States who can be inspired to commit acts of violence. It is this blending of homegrown violent extremism with the foreign fighter ideology that is today's latest adaptation of the threat.

ISIL has proven to be relentless and continues to terrorize individuals in Syria and Iraq, including Westerners. We are concerned about the possibility of homegrown extremists becoming radicalized by information available on the Internet. ISIL's widespread reach through the Internet and social media is most concerning as the group has proven dangerously competent at employing such tools for its nefarious strategy. ISIL utilizes high-quality, traditional media platforms, as well as widespread social media campaigns to propagate its extremist ideas. Recently released propaganda has included various English language publications circulated via social media. Several videos of ISIL-held hostages and videos glorifying ISIL members have also been released.

As a communications tool, the Internet remains a critical node for terror groups to exploit. Recently, a group of five individuals was arrested for knowingly and willingly conspiring and attempting to provide material support and resources to designated foreign terrorist organizations active in Syria and Iraq. Much of their conspiracy occurred via the Internet. We remain concerned about recent calls to action by ISIL and its supporters on violent extremist web forums that could potentially motivate homegrown extremists to conduct attacks here at home. Online supporters of ISIL have used various social media platforms to call for retaliation against the U.S. In one case, an Ohio-based man was arrested in January after he stated his intent to conduct an attack on the U.S. Capitol building. The individual used a Twitter account to post statements, videos, and other content indicating support for ISIL.

Echoing other terrorist groups, ISIL has advocated for lone wolf attacks. This past January, ISIL released a video via social media networking sites reiterating the group's support of lone offender attacks in Western countries. This video specifically advocates for attacks against soldiers, law enforcement and intelligence members. Several incidents have occurred in the United States and Europe over the last few months that indicate this "call to arms" has resonated among ISIL supporters and sympathizers.

Our partners in Australia, Canada, France, and the United Kingdom (UK) have recently disrupted plotting and, unfortunately, had security officers attacked by individuals linked to ISIL or other forms of violent extremism. A French national, who took hostages in Paris and shot and killed a policewoman in early January, claimed he was an ISIL supporter. In December 2014, another French national entered a police station in France and began stabbing police officers before being killed by police. Two separate attacks in Canada in October 2014 targeted Canadian soldiers. Additionally, in September and October, the UK and Australian authorities separately thwarted attacks targeting local law enforcement.

Soon after the January attacks in France, authorities in Belgium conducted a raid against several individuals who were allegedly planning an attack against police personnel. These individuals purportedly had ties to ISIL and allegedly had some connections to the individuals responsible for the attacks in Paris. Our European partners remain on heightened alert and continue to take the necessary steps to mitigate imminent threats. Additionally, last week an individual in Copenhagen attacked a café and a synagogue before dying in a shootout with law enforcement. The individual reportedly pledged allegiance to ISIL before conducting the attack.

The recent events in Europe also underscore our need to remain vigilant here at home, as these small scale attacks are feasible within the United States. Individuals inspired by foreign terrorist groups could quietly arm themselves with the expertise and tools to carry out an attack. Community and world events may trigger one of these individuals to take action. As we've seen with the highly publicized events of the attack on the military at the Tomb of the Unknown Soldier in Canada and the hostage situation at a café in Australia, any attempt at an act of terror will attract international media attention. We remain concerned these types of events, which were widely broadcast, could inspire "copy cat" attacks.

The idea of carrying out small scale attacks is not new. In addition to ISIL's online propaganda encouraging attacks on Western interests in any manner possible, al-Qa'ida in the Arabian Peninsula (AQAP) has also promoted conducting attacks using simple and inexpensive methods. AQAP continues to pose a threat to the United States and our interests overseas. AQAP's online English magazine *Inspire* advocates for lone wolves to conduct attacks against the U.S. homeland and Western targets and once again highlighted some ways to do so in the recent edition released on December 24, 2014. As with the previous editions, the magazine encourages homegrown violent extremists to carry out small arms attacks and provides detailed "how to" instructions for constructing and deploying a successful bomb.

In conjunction with our domestic and foreign partners, we are rigorously collecting and analyzing intelligence information as it pertains to the ongoing threat posed by ISIL, AQAP, and other foreign terrorist organizations. Given the global impact of the Syria and Iraq conflicts, regular engagement with our domestic and foreign partners concerning foreign fighters is critical.

The FBI, along with our local, state, and federal partners, is utilizing all investigative techniques and methods to combat the threat these individuals may pose to the United States. We must maintain robust information sharing and close collaboration with our state, local, and federal partners. Individuals who are affiliated with a foreign terrorist organization, inspired by a foreign terrorist organization, or who are self-radicalized are living in their communities. We at the FBI recognize it is our responsibility to share information pertaining to ongoing or emerging threats immediately. Our local and state partners rely on this intelligence to conduct their investigations and maintain the safety of their communities. It is our responsibility to provide them with the information and resources to keep their communities out of harm's way. In each of the FBI's 56 Field Offices, the Joint Terrorism Task Forces serve as a vital mechanism for information sharing among our partners. Together with our local, state, and federal partners, we are committed to combating the threat from homegrown violent extremists and ensuring the safety of the American public.

The FBI continues to pursue increased information sharing, efforts to combat radicalization, and exchanges regarding community outreach programs and policing strategies.

Chairman Sensenbrenner, Ranking Member Lee, and Committee Members, I thank you for this opportunity to testify concerning the threat foreign fighters and homegrown extremists pose to the homeland. I am happy to answer any questions you might have.

Mr. SENSENBRENNER. Without objection.
Sheriff Stanek?

TESTIMONY OF RICHARD W. STANEK, SHERIFF, HENNEPIN COUNTY, MINNEAPOLIS, MN

Sheriff STANEK. ——
Mr. SENSENBRENNER. Could you please turn your mic on, Sheriff?
Sheriff STANEK. I'm sorry.
Mr. SENSENBRENNER. And we will reset the clock.
Sheriff STANEK. Well, thank you, Chairman Sensenbrenner and Congresswoman Jackson Lee, for you generous invitation to testify this morning about our community engagement efforts in the Twin Cities and, in particular, our outreach efforts to the Somali Diaspora Community.

I'm Sheriff Rich Stanek from Hennepin County, Minneapolis, Minnesota, a very diverse county with 1.2 million residents; 425,000 of those residents are non-Caucasian. We have 40,000 Oromo, 35,000 Liberians, and nearly 100,000 Somali residents living in Hennepin County; the largest Somali population in the Nation.

I have 32 years of policing experience and I currently serve on the National Sheriffs and Major County Sheriffs Association executive boards representing our Nation's sheriffs.

Mr. Chair and Members, just last week I joined our United States Attorney, Andy Luger and other community leaders from Minnesota to participate in a White House Summit on Countering Violent Extremism. We learned firsthand in late 2008 about the reality of radicalization when we had dozens of young men radicalized by al-Shabaab and leave the Twin Cities to fight in Somalia. Several have been confirmed killed fighting for al-Shabaab, including the first confirmed suicide bomber from the United States, Shirwa Ahmend.

Mr. Chairman, as one of the Committee Members pointed out this morning, we also had Douglas McAuthur McCain, the first American killed in Syria fighting with ISIL. Most of these young men had never seen Somalia or Syria, they only knew of their American lives. Their parents were shocked that their sons would return to the place that they had so desperately fled.

The threat of radicalization from designated terrorist organizations like al-Shababb or ISIL, has become even more invasive; YouTube videos and chat rooms, Facebook pages with links to increasingly violent radical online programs, training, and ideology. And these threats are real.

Just this week, al-Shababb released another propaganda video on YouTube mentioning the Mall of America in Bloomington, Minnesota, one of the largest cities in my county, encouraging al-Shababb followers to act out.

Now, Mr. Chairman, Members, this is a marked change in the message from recruiting people to train overseas to recruiting Americans to train and act out here in the homeland; akin to a lone wolf.

In response, we issued a joint media statement and public messaging, included the participation of local, state, and Federal law enforcement, as well as the Mall of America Security, a private corporation. We have developed these public-private partnerships that also include the Somali Community leaders, educators, and member of the business community, as well as faith leaders, to strengthen the public safety fabric of our community.

Our efforts at first were to respond, but now we work to prevent and work to intervene. We help community leaders and family members identify the behaviors that can be cause for concern; such as withdrawal from family and normal social circles, accessing radical religious or Jihadist websites, forming close partnership within a small group of likeminded people, or obtaining large sums of money, conducting fundraising efforts, and acquiring travel documents amongst others.

We are concerned, Mr. Chairman and others, about young people in isolation who cut themselves off from their family and their support networks. So we encourage parents, mothers and fathers, educators, business, and faith leaders, to close their own generational and cultural gaps and reach out to at-risk youth. We all share a common mission of protecting our kids and our future.

Mr. Chair and Members, at first, traditional methods for building communities of trust weren't working. We had language and cultural barriers that required new strategies: translations were difficult at best; men didn't want women at meetings; certain groups were in opposition to other groups; The greatest barrier of all, though, Somalis were distrustful of law enforcement because in their home country law enforcement often operates as the oppressive arm of government.

The key to overcoming these barriers was the one-on-one personal relationships between a gentleman named Imam Roble and myself. Imam Roble was introduced and offered his prayer for world peace at the opening of the White House CVE Summit just last week. Others trusted us because he trusted us. He became our sponsor in the community, personally asking members to attend One Day Citizen, academies tailored to the Somali community. And we let everyone know we would be working with everyone; the elders, the religious leaders, women, and youth. We hired the first sworn Somali Deputy Sheriff in Minnesota, Halssan Hussein. We added a Somali community member to our Community Engagement Team, Abdi Mohamed.

A great example of our new level of engagement. A Somali woman on our Community Advisory Board assisted us in adopting a new policy on religious head coverings, hijabs, in our jail.

For me and law enforcement officers like me across this great country, fulfilling our Oath of Office means more than respect. We protect the privacy and the civil liberties of all residents in addition to their safety. And, for us, this is what it means to serve and protect.

Mr. Chair and Members, violent extremism is a local threat. Local law enforcement will be the first to respond and we should be on the front line to educate and strengthen our communities, and to prevent or disrupt these threats. Our local law enforcement efforts coincide with the White House National Strategy for Counterterrorism to protect our local communities in ways that are consistent with our values as a Nation and as a people.

By protecting the civil rights and liberties, we are strengthening our communities and building resiliency.

Mr. Chairman and Members, we are presenting our American model of self-government, and the rule of law, an alternative to the radical message and ideology, a model of freedom and opportunity, education, dignity, and hope.

Mr. Chair and Members, thank you very much for the opportunity to testify here this morning.

[The prepared statement of Mr. Stanek follows:]

RICHARD W. STANEK
HENNEPIN COUNTY SHERIFF

U.S. House Judiciary
Subcommittee on Crime, Terrorism, Homeland Security, and Investigations
Thursday, February 26, 2015
Testimony by Sheriff Richard W. Stanek

Thank you, Chairman Sensenbrenner and Congresswoman Jackson Lee, for your invitation to testify this morning about our Community Engagement efforts in the Twin Cities, and, in particular, our outreach to the Somali Diaspora Community.

I am Sheriff Rich Stanek from Hennepin County, Minnesota. a very diverse County with 1.2 million residents:
- 425,000 are non-Caucasian;
- Our population is growing and demographics are changing every day; and
- We have 40,000 Oromo, 35,000 Liberians, and nearly 100,000 Somali residents living in Hennepin County.

Mr. Chair and Members, last week. I joined our U.S. Attorney, and other law enforcement and community leaders from Minnesota in participating in the White House Summit on Countering Violent Extremism. We learned firsthand in late 2008 about the reality of radicalization when we had dozens of young men radicalized by Al Shabaab, and leave the Twin Cities to fight in Somalia. Several have been confirmed killed fighting for Al Shabaab. At least 2 were suicide bombers, including the first confirmed suicide bomber from the United States, Shirwa Ahmed. Most of these young men had never seen Somalia, they knew only of their American lives. The parents were shocked their sons would return to the place they had so desperately fled.

The threat of radicalization from designated terrorist organizations, whether from Al Shabaab or ISIS/ISIL, has become even more invasive: YouTube videos, chat rooms, ordinary looking Facebook pages with links to increasingly violent radical on-line programs, training and ideology.

And these threats are real: just this week, Al Shabaab released another propaganda video on YouTube mentioning the Mall of America in Bloomington, Minnesota (one of the largest cities in Hennepin County) encouraging Al Shabaab followers to act out. This is a marked change in the message: from recruiting people to train overseas, to recruiting Americans to train and act out here in the homeland, akin to a lone wolf.

In response we issued a joint media statement that included the participation of local, state and federal law enforcement and Mall of America Security, a private corporation. We have developed these public-private partnerships that also include Somali Community leaders: educators, members of the business community, and faith leaders – to strengthen the public safety fabric of our communities.

Our efforts at first were to respond, but now we work to prevent and intervene. We work to educate community leaders and family members about the threat of radicalization, and help them identify the behaviors that can be cause for concern:

- Withdrawal from family and normal social circles.
- Accessing radical religious or jihadist websites.
- Forming close relationships within a small group of likeminded people.
- Obtaining large sums of money – conducting fundraising efforts.
- Acquiring travel documents.

We are concerned about young people in isolation, who cut themselves off from their family and support network. So we encourage parents – mothers and fathers – educators, the business community, community leaders and faith leaders, to close their own generational and cultural gaps, and reach out to at-risk youth. We all share a common mission in protecting our kids and our future.

At first, traditional methods for building communities of trust weren't working. We had language and cultural barriers that required new strategies:

- Translations were difficult at best.
- Men didn't want women at meetings.
- Certain groups were in opposition to other groups.
- The greatest barrier of all: Somalis were distrustful of law enforcement -- because in their home country law enforcement often operates as the arm of an oppressive government.

The key to overcoming these barriers <u>was the one-on-one personal relationship</u> between Imam Roble and me. We've been friends for more than 5 years now, and any success the Sheriff's Office has had in engaging the Somali Diaspora in Hennepin County is due largely to Imam Roble and his guidance and leadership. After many conversations, he agreed to help us, and leant credibility to our efforts. Others trusted us, because he trusted us. He became our sponsor in the community, personally asking members to attend One Day Citizen- Academies customized for the Somali community. We let everyone know that we would be working with everyone: Elders, Religious leaders, Women and Youth.

We followed up with those early connections, and hired the first sworn Somali Deputy Sheriff in Minnesota, Haissan Hussein. We added a Somali community member as a civilian in our Community Engagement Team, Abdi Mohamed. Imam Roble serves as a member of our Community Advisory Board.

A great example of our new level of engagement: A Somali woman on our Community Advisory Board assisted us in adopting a new policy on religious head coverings (hijabs) in the jail. This

new policy is just one way for my office to show the community that we are not only listening, we are acting.

For me and law enforcement officers like me across the Country, fulfilling our Oath of Office means more than respect, we protect the privacy and civil liberties of all residents, in addition to their safety. For us, this is what it means to serve and protect.

In Hennepin County, we continue our hiring efforts to create an Agency as diverse as the County, to better reflect the community we serve, and to break down communication and cultural barriers. Each contact is an opportunity for us to demonstrate our commitment to building trusting and lasting relationships – to create resiliency.

With Imam Roble's guidance, I've learned, the most important member of our Community Engagement Team is ...me. Our community leaders want to be respected. This isn't a job to delegate to someone else but a responsibility shared throughout the entire Agency, starting at the top.

Violent extremism is a local threat; local law enforcement will be the first to respond and we should be at the front line to educate and strengthen our communities, and prevent or disrupt these threats.

Our local law enforcement efforts coincide with the White House National Strategy for Counterterrorism, to protect our local communities in ways that are "consistent with our values as a nation and as a people:"
- By addressing the needs of residents,
- By hearing their concerns,
- By encouraging participation and community ownership.
- By educating residents about our criminal justice system, and
- By protecting their civil rights and liberties, ...

We are strengthening our communities and building resiliency. We are presenting our American model of self-government and the rule of law, an alternative to the radical message and ideology, a model of freedom and opportunity, education, dignity and hope.

Thank you Mr. Chair and Members of the Committee, I'd be happy to take questions.

Mr. SENSENBRENNER. Well, thank you both for very on-point testimony.

And Sheriff, let me say I particularly appreciate your outlined type of community outreach to basically identify people who might become radicalized by sitting in front a computer. I think that this is very important particularly in light of the FBI Director's admonition that there are ISIL cells in every state in the country. It is a problem that we face in our local communities, and anyone who thinks that they are immune of the reach of these types of radicals because they live far away from New York or Washington D.C., I think,is deluding themselves.

I guess that the best thing the citizens can do is, if you see something, say something and let law enforcement know about it. And the fact that the threat against the Mall of America was not something that was picked up through any kind of classified intelligence information but the radicals put it right up on the Internet, shows how embolden they are in terms of being able to try to perpetrate giving people who might not be in face-to-face contact with them, some very bad ideas on how to harm America and how to harm Americans. You know, I hope that what you have been doing in the Twin Cities is something that can be expanded nationwide where these undercover cells are. So thank you.

I don't have any questions of you. I think you hit all of the bases, but I do have some questions for Mr. Steinbach.

We know that several U.S. citizens and U.S. persons have traveled to Syria. They usually go through Turkey; they sneak across the borders. How are you able to track these people and, I guess of greater concern, how are you able to track not only people with U.S. passports but people with passports from VISA waiver countries who have gone to Syria who might be returning or going to the United States?

Mr. STEINBACH. Sure. So I think it is a complicated answer. There are lots of ways we identify potential travelers: human source, technical means, strong partnerships, particularly with our European partners state and local level, partnerships. It has got to be a multitude of resources of plight toward the threat. We don't get that threat right all the time. We don't catch every single one that crosses, that leaves the country. As you know, it is not illegal to depart the United States, so we don't track folks departing in the United States, and they have become very smart about going to European destinations to mask their travel. So we have to stay on top of it. So we have to, again, use a multitude of resources including foreign partners who stay on top of it.

Mr. SENSENBRENNER. Do you have the necessary authorities to be able to deal with these people should they attempt to come back to the United States?

Mr. STEINBACH. Absolutely.

If an individual travels over to Syria in support of ISIL, on neutral front or any foreign terrorist organization, 2339, U.S. 18-2339, show support to terrorism, is a good tool to use and it is an effective tool.

Mr. SENSENBRENNER. Let me get to people who come from VISA waiver countries which are primarily Western European. Are you able to track whether any of the people who don't need VISAs, in an attempt to fly to the United States are able to be caught before they arrive and if they are not caught before they arrive at the time of the airport that they are entering into the United States?

Mr. STEINBACH. So, yes and no, sir.

The knowns, and so I think Ranking Member Lee mentioned the numbers and the volume of travelers. That is the volume of travelers going to Syria that we know about. There is a, an order of magnitude that is unknown to European allies. The known members, the known travelers, they are watch listed appropriately. So whether they are from a VISA waiver country or not they are watch listed appropriately and we can spot them before they come to the United States. Those unknown individuals that the European allies are not aware of are not watch listed, that is the problem and that is where the challenge is.

Mr. SENSENBRENNER. Okay. Thank you very much.

The gentle woman from Texas, Ms. Jackson Lee.

Ms. JACKSON LEE. Let me thank both of you for the excellent testimony that you have given and the partnership, though it is not an established partnership, between local government sheriff and the FBI, Mr. Steinbach, is evident that it is crucial.

Let me say to the Sheriff and to my colleagues, as Sheriff Stanek mentioned, he was in Washington last week and I am particularly grateful that you have accepted our invitation to come back this week.

So let me go to you first. You made a very important statement that should be reinforced. And I think Mr. Steinbach, when I question him, will likewise reinforce it. In this country, violent extremism is a local threat as evidenced by FBI Director Comcy as well, about ISIL cells and others. So you were in the eye of the storm.

Earlier this week, the terrorist organization al-Shababb posted a video declaring that Westgate was just a beginning. Al-Shabaab and al-Qaeda, affiliate based in Somalia, took credit for the 2013 attack on Westgate shopping mall in Nairobi; we know how vicious and vile that was and how many lost their lives. The video goes on to mention the Mall of America in Bloomington, Minnesota which you have spoken of.

So I want to pointedly ask you, do we not have a due responsibility? The threat came right to your doorsteps and I'd like you to offer either your assessment of the tools that you have, fusion centers, joint terrorism centers, collaboration, with that threat coming to your doorstep even if someone would argue that it is simply a threat with no ability to be implemented. I always believe that caution is the better of the game. But match that with your answer about the outreach and, as that video came out, the potential of the outreach in relationships to get information from the community in which we speak; the Somalian community.

Sheriff?

Sheriff STANEK. Sure.

Well, thank you Congresswoman Jackson Lee. You are not the first one to ask me that question this week, so I appreciate that.

Look, this—we have set. This propaganda video put out by ISIL mentioning the Mall of America and just that. It is not the first time it has been mentioned. Our resiliency in Minnesota with local law enforcement, my Federal law enforcement partners, is very strong. We train, we exercise, we plan and prepare incessantly hoping that something bad never happens but knowing full well that each and every day across this country and across this world it does. But we are prepared.

We worked through the Joint Terrorism Taskforce with the FBI, we work with our private sector partners like I mentioned, add on that the Mall of America is a private security force but they work hand-in-hand with the Bloomington Police Department, our Sheriff's Office, our Federal law enforcement partners. Our fusion center in Minnesota is robust and does a great job day in and day out getting the information out to me as the Chief Law Enforcement Officer in my county.

Ms. JACKSON LEE. My time is running out. Go to the next part of it, the outreach part and how that plays a role. And then I have a question for Mr. Steinbach. So I am watching the clock, but thank you.

Sheriff STANEK. Great. So, I'm sorry.

Just yesterday afternoon, before coming out here, I had lunch with member of the Somalia Diaspora community. We talked about the Mall of America as well as other things. They renounced what they saw in that video. That would not have happened several years ago. They wouldn't know how to respond. We work with them day-in and day-out to empower them to understand what is happening in their community with their young men and young women so that these radicalization efforts do not happen. It is about building long-term communities of trust and a respectful partnership that is enduring.

Ms. JACKSON LEE. Thank you so very much.

Mr. Steinbach, let me thank you for your work and thank the FBI for that excellent work in New York just in the last 24 to 48 hours.

Very quickly, I'm concerned about the no-fly and—let me just say foreign fighters. And we are looking at legislation dealing with making sure our lists are accurate. But, frame for us again the extent of the potential foreign fighters coming to the United States. And then comment on any FBI efforts that deals with the extremism as it relates to women, which is increasing, as related by the Denver young ladies who I think the FBI was very much involved in; and certainly an article that I just read about a young woman in Scotland who was a perfect teenager and now has become known as the darling recruiter of women into extremism. How is the FBI sectioned, has a separate section or knowing that this is a particular issue that it must deal with?

Mr. STEINBACH. So really quickly. So foreign fighter is a problem but it is a small problem compared to our European partners. The larger problem is that population of HVEs inspired—those individuals who were frustrated travelers, denied travelers don't have the means to travel. Foreign fighters, small. The larger populous and the larger concern is much larger. ISIL and others are looking to recruit that part. They know they can't travel so what they are doing is they are putting out a very effective propaganda message through social media, through lots of platforms saying "Hey, if you can't come to Syria, doing something in the U.S. or Western countries."

That social media outreach is focused on those who use social media; our youth. So you find the trend over the last year or so has been a decreasing age group that are being recruited both male and female, as well as you are seeing more females, younger females, attracted to this message.

Mr. SENSENBRENNER. The gentle woman's time has expired. The gentleman from Ohio, Mr. Chabot.

Mr. CHABOT. Thank you, Mr. Chairman.

Mr. Steinbach, let me begin by commending you and the FBI for your work in apprehending that 20-year old radicalized individual who intended to attack the capitol building across the street. This was sort of near and dear to me because he was from my district, went to a local high school there in the mosque that he allegedly attended, is about a quarter of a mile from the place I had my first job and is two miles from the home that I lived in for 30 years and lived in that, within two miles, for 50 years now. So this is right in the heart of where we come from.

My first question was, he claimed to have attended that mosque, and it is relatively close to where he would have grown up et cetera. The coverage back home on television, the people from the mosque that were on TV were asked about him, said, "Well, we never saw him. We don't know anything about him." Is that something that has been looked into up to this point? Do we know if he was connected to that Mosque or not?

Mr. STEINBACH. Let me be careful about talking about an ongoing investigation——

Mr. CHABOT. I understand.

Mr. STEINBACH [continuing]. But I will say that, yes, we have strong understanding with our local partners there, state and locals, as to how as radicalization beginnings, what his intent was. So we are pretty comfortable understanding that individual.

Mr. SENSENBRENNER. In that it was or wasn't connected to that mosque?

Mr. STEINBACH. So, again, I don't want to get into the specifics of the investigation. I would say to back it up in general and talk about HVEs in general. I will say the majority of the radicalization proces now, though varied as it is, we are finding the majority is online and the Internet.

Mr. CHABOT. Right.

And clearly it looked at the majority of what the input came and the motivation was online and as you indicated that seems to be happening more and more frequently.

Sheriff Stanek, let me ask you. I also want to commend you for your work in reaching out to the Somali community in your area and forging a strong bond—enforcement in the Somali Diaspora and the work you are doing to continue your hiring efforts in order to create a more diverse agency in those types of things.

Let me ask you about—there has been some controversy about a spokeswoman at the state department who has made some interesting proposition about, you know, we need to find more jobs for these folks and, if we can do that, then they won't end up killing us; for lack of a better term. Her quote exactly was "We need to go after the root causes that lead people to join these groups whether it is lack of opportunity for jobs or whatever, we can help them build their economies so they can have job opportunities for these people."

And you know, with an unemployment rate of 3.6 which is 2 Percent under the national average in Minnesota and congratulations on that. Do you believe that if we had created more jobs for the dozens of young men who were radicalized by al-Shababb and became suicide bombers in Somalia that they would have chosen a different path?

Sheriff STANEK. Yeah, Mr. Chairman and Congressman Chabot, thank you very much for that question.

You know, I think that is only one part of the equation. I think that is not the only way that these individuals thrive and grow in our community. Minnesota prides itself on a very diverse community. Many of us in Minnesota are immigrants. I come from a Polish heritage, second generation. A lot of folks. But education, jobs, the economy, only one part of it. The other part is also understanding the American criminal justice system, understanding our culture, and for us to understand what they bring to the table. We have worked extremely hard on this. It is not easy. It is about those long-term trust and relationships that we are working every day to build.

Mr. CHABOT. Thank you.

And just to follow up and I am almost out of time here. As Chairman now of the Small Business Committee and having served on that Committee and this one for 19 years now, and I am all for job creation and getting this economy moving and we can do that by lessening the regulations on small businesses and reforming the tax code and a whole range of things, but anybody that thinks that a job program is going to go a long way toward solving our problem with these radicalized folks in this country or over there, I think that is not a very correct way of thinking about this. I mean these people are deadly serious. They have a job and that is beheading people and torturing people and, you know, their mentality is, you know, convert or die and we got to defeat them.

Thank you.

Mr. SENSENBRENNER. The gentleman's time has expired.

The gentleman from Michigan, Mr. Conyers.

Mr. CONYERS. Thank you, Mr. Chairman.

I want to commend the testimony we have heard here today from these gentlemen and it is, to me, very important that I compliment Sheriff Stanek because you anticipated the very set of questions I was going to put to someone that is right there on the ground as to how do you interact and relate to people of a different faith, many of whom are very nervous about elected officials and law enforcement officials particularly. And yours, that you have discussed here today and the interaction that you have made, not only with the community but what the leaders of their community, are extremely critical. And I think it is a step-by-step instruction manual for local law enforcement officials everywhere in this country to follow.

Are there any considerations about this part of our discussion here today that you would like to add to?

Sheriff STANEK. Mr. Chairman and Congressman Conyers, you are absolutely correct and thank you very much.

The men and women who work in my Sheriff's Office as well as my partner law enforcement agencies in Minnesota really appreciate that. In fact, as you know, Minnesota, the Minneapolis areas, was selected as one of the three pilot cities across the U.S., in Boston, Los Angeles, and Minneapolis, to share what we learned. Unfortunately, we learned as a result of some, you know, tragic incidents with Douglas McCain and Shirwa Ahmed but we fully intend on helping our local law enforcement partners understand what we can do. Race, ethnicity, gender have not place in terms of policing. We treat everybody equally and, like I said, we not only respect, we protect the civil rights and liberties.

Mr. CONYERS. Well, that is what I think we need to get out because there is an understandable dichotomy between people of different faiths and religions relating to law enforcement and elected officials. And I think you have set the pace for how it ought to be done. And I hope that we can somehow get, incorporate, your experiences into messages that we here in Washington, all the members of the Federal legislature, get out all the people in our country.

Director Steinbach, I am, with respect to the threat posed by the Islamic State and other terrorist organizations, you state that the FBI along with our local, state, and Federal partners is utilizing all investigative techniques and methods to combat the threat these individuals may pose to the United States. Now, when you say Federal partners, do you include the Department of Homeland Security?

Mr. STEINBACH. Yes, sir.

Mr. CONYERS. Well, I noticed that in your testimony on February the eleventh before Homeland Security, you referred specifically and explicitly to that. Isn't that correct?

Mr. STEINBACH. I am going to leave that to you—I assume so, sir. I can't recall.

Mr. CONYERS. Well, I can help you. You did.

Mr. STEINBACH. Okay.

Mr. CONYERS. But you didn't mention that today. And, as you know, in very shortly we are going to be out of funding for that. Do you have any recommendations or views about the funding of the Department of Homeland Security?

Mr. STEINBACH. No, sir. I will not comment on that.

Mr. CONYERS. How come?

Mr. STEINBACH. Sir, I think it is a political question and I am going to stay out of that. My job as the Assistant Director of Counterterrorism is to lead the FBI efforts in counterterrorism.

Mr. CONYERS. Well, I tried.

Mr. SENSENBRENNER. The gentleman's time has expired.

The gentleman from Idaho, Mr. Labrador.

Mr. LABRADOR. Thank you very much. And I want to thank both of you for being here today. I want to thank you for your service and for the good work you are doing for the people of the United States and in your communities.

Mr. Steinbach, in your written testimony you mention that ISIL's online program propaganda efforts is a threat to Western interests. How is the FBI approaching spread of ISIL's online presence?

Mr. STEINBACH. So I think it is not just the FBI, it is the whole of government including state and local partners like the Sheriff

45

here. We have to approach it from a counter messaging perspective where we look to counter violent extremists efforts at the local level in particular, like the Sheriff mentioned, a larger counter messaging narrative, and then, of course, we have to look at from an investigative point-of-view, from an intelligence collecting point-of-view. Find out where they are at and be where they are at in social media and on the Internet.

Mr. LABRADOR. Sheriff, what are you doing at the local level to counter the, especially the propaganda that is on the Internet?

Sheriff STANEK. Well, Mr. Chairman and Congressman Labrador, you know, we try and change the narrative of this propaganda. Like I said, it is not the first time the Mall of America, an iconic institution, happens to be located in Minnesota, has been mentioned. We go to the community itself and help empower them. We look to the young people like the organization called Ka Joog, Muhammad Farah and others were out here last week with us, where Imam Roble and the religious leaders or some of the business people like Mr. Bihi and others who every day are out in the community. They are reflective of the community and they work with local law enforcement to help change that narrative, help the young people understand, talking with the moms, the Somali mothers of these young men and women who for some reason choose, like I said, to be radicalized, maybe go overseas, maybe act out here, but we work with them. It is not easy. Like I said, it is a long-term trusted relationship, it is not just a conversation, it is a discussion we come back to the table time and time and time again.

Mr. LABRADOR. Thank you.

Mr. Steinbach, we know that the problems we had in Brooklyn, that the persons who were arrested were not American citizens, they were legal permanent residents. Is that correct?

Mr. STEINBACH. Yes, sir.

Mr. LABRADOR. Now, are we finding that most of our problems are with non-citizens, with people that are here illegally, or are you finding more problems with actual young kids who were born in the United States?

Mr. STEINBACH. So I think an interesting fact on some of the individuals that we investigate for support to ISIL is the lack of a singular profile. We find citizens, legal permanent resident aliens, some folks that are overstaying their VISA. There is actually quite a diversity of those individuals who, for one reason or another, stated an intent to harm the United States.

Mr. LABRADOR. So do you think this is a growing threat? Do you think that the Brooklyn situation is representative of a growing threat of the United States?

Mr. STEINBACH. I believe that it is a good example of what the threat looks like which is individuals who perhaps began their intellectual curiosity looking online, at some point were radicalized before, but became more radicalized online, focused their efforts to do something to travel overseas. If they can't travel overseas, to conduct an attack on the U.S. We are seeing that play more and more often. So I would say it is probably a good cross section of some of the cases we have.

Mr. LABRADOR. Are you finding a growing threat also of people coming from Western Europe and other areas to the United States who have these radicalized ideas?

Mr. STEINBACH. So I don't if it is a growing threat. I don't know if we see an uptick in Western Europeans coming to the United States to conduct an attack or do some type of operation. Again, it is a cross section of individuals, those who have been born and raised in the United States, those that are first generation residents, legal permanent residents, those who have come in and have overstayed their VISA. It really is a lack of a profile on their status that is remarkable in this threat.

Mr. LABRADOR. How do you think we can then combat that? Do you have any suggestions for us here in Congress about some things that we should be doing and thinking about?

Mr. STEINBACH. If I were to comment on one area where I think we are most concerned about as an organization, as an intelligence community, it is on the idea of ''Going Dark'' which I think I mentioned in my testimony.

So there are essentially three paradigm shifts. After 9/11, the Internet, and this third paradigm shift being social media. And the ability of sympathizers, recruits, to use social media effectively is a concern for us. And the concern is that, with the number of social media companies, with encryption, we are continuing to ''Go Dark'' both as a law enforcement community, as an intelligence community. So I would ask Congress to look seriously toward updating CALEA and laws and legislation to allow us to lawfully intercept. When we have got the right through the FSK or through the criminal courts to intercept communication content, I would ask that we receive help from Congress to go down that road. It is a concern, and we continue to lose more and more ability to see the content lawfully.

Mr. LABRADOR. Thank you.

Mr. SENSENBRENNER. The gentleman's time has expired.

The gentle woman from California, Ms. Chu.

Ms. CHU. Sheriff Stanek, the countering violent extremism program is designed in part to encourage individuals to provide law enforcement with information deemed suspicious or predictive of violent extremism. I have heard from the Muslim American community who have concerns that the program is largely focused on them and that it can be stigmatizing, can lead to distrust between the American Muslim community and law enforcement. As someone who has worked directly on these issues, could you share your approach to building trust and ensuring that your community is safe or minorities are not isolated? And, could you also describe law enforcement to practices that have not worked in the past?

Sheriff STANEK. Yeah. Mr. Chairman and Congresswoman Chu, thank you very much for that question.

You are correct. Countering Violent Extremism, CVE, is different that Community Engagement Techniques, CET. And so we do not mix the two. You cannot, shall not, mix the two. If members of the Diaspora community think that your community engagement techniques are not nothing more than a front for intelligence gathering to counter violent extremism, that is a problem. You get at countering violent extremism by building strong relationships in the community through community engagement techniques. And I want to be clear about that.

Again, the strategy that local law enforcement uses is akin to community anointed policing concepts like we use with gangs and other things as we have fought them across this country. And they are age-old, tried and true techniques and practices in which local law enforcement works every day with those communities to help them understand, and, like I said earlier, to help empower them to do for themselves and be responsive to local law enforcement.

Ms. CHU. Thank you for that.

And, Director Steinbach, what steps are the FBI taking to ensure that the CVE programs do not stigmatize Islam or single out Muslim Americans?

Mr. STEINBACH. I think the Sheriff alluded to it best, ma'am.

Community Countering Violent Extremism is best left to the local level. I shouldn't be sitting here in D.C. dictating how Sheriff Stanek is going to involve his community in that outreach and that program. We need to, at the Federal Government level, empower them but push it down to the community level, which is why I think you saw last week Los Angeles, Boston, and Minneapolis come and kind of lay out their models. I think each model has to be individually tailored based on the needs of the community.

But I really think that CVE efforts needs to be pushed out to the local level, much like DARE. Let the community, not only the police, but community centers, religious institutions, the schools, they have to be intimately involved. They are the best place to handle that.

Ms. CHU. Okay, thank you.

Sheriff, 2 weeks ago in North Carolina, three young American Muslims were murdered execution style by a neighbor who, it is widely documented, expressed deeep hatred of Muslims as well as other religions. As you might imagine, there are many people in this country who have formed bigoted views of all Muslims as a result of ISIL. In fact, after 9/11 the number of anti-Muslim hate crimes increased nearly 500-fold. And in the year since, annual hate crimes have hovered in the 100 to 150 range; about five times higher than the pre-9/11 rate. What steps are being taken to ensure that hate crimes against American Muslims do not occur?

Sheriff STANEK. Yeah. Mr. Chair and Congresswoman, we work extensively with the Department of Homeland Security and the Office of Civil Rights and Liberties, reaching out to our Muslim community helping them understand what their rights are, where to complain.

We just dealt with a mosque in one of our local communities. They wanted to build a mosque. That suburban community said no, for whatever reason it was. We followed up with the United States Attorney. He was very bold, he was very straightforward. He sued that local community to help them have a better understanding, I think, of what it means for religious freedom and to be able to do what they want to do within the bounds of law.

That mosque is now—the groundbreaking is next week. I will be attending proudly representing local law enforcement. That is a great example of doing things the right way for the right reason and not discriminating.

Ms. CHU. Thank you. I yield back.

Mr. GOHMERT [presiding]. The gentle lady yields back.

This time the Chair yields to the gentleman from Texas, Judge Poe.

Mr. POE. Appreciate the Chairman.

Thank you, gentlemen, for being here.

As the Chairman indicated, I used to be a criminal court judge in Texas and a prosecutor. I just give you that by way of background in the criminal justice area.

A hundred and fifty Americans have traveled abroad, recruited by ISIS. How were they recruited?

Mr. STEINBACH. I am sorry, sir?

Mr. POE. How were they recruited? The so-called 150 that have been radicalized and gone abroad, how were they recruited?

Mr. STEINBACH. So not 150 have traveled abroad. That is our category. So that includes a bucket of those who have tried to travel, those who have been killed, those who have been arrested. But broadly, that 150ish number, I would say there is a variety of means. If I had to categorize one method over the other, I would say the Internet or social media probably ranks highest, but there is also friends and associates. But I would say the Internet and social media probably is the overriding.

Mr. POE. Would you agree with that, Sheriff?

Sheriff STANEK. You know, Mr. Chairman and Congressman, I do. That, as well as I think extended families. A lot of folks in my community, again, maybe we are just a little bit different because I have got that large Somalia population, but a lot of them, a lot of them have extended family back in around the Horn of Africa.

Mr. POE. I want to specifically talk about ISIS and other foreign terrorist organizations. With that label that we give them, not a terrorist that somebody may just say, "Well, that is a terrorist out there in the fruited plain." But specifically, foreign terrorist organizations and ISIS and their recruitment.

The Section 219 of the Immigration Nationality Act states that "It is unlawful to provide a designated foreign terrorist organization with material support or resources including property tangible or intangible or services." I'm sure you have heard that, read that before.

Twitter seems to be one of the avenues of social media where individuals are radicalized or recruited through public Twitter sites. I am not talking about the private chatter. I am talking about the public. And they use propaganda, recruitment, and they raise money on Twitter. Would both of you weigh-in on the obligation of Twitter if any, in your opinion—I'm asking your opinion, not a legal opinion, of being more proactive on taking down those sites? After all, you just said they had been recruited by social media and that is just one of the many others; Facebook and YouTube seem to be a fairly good job of taking down those individual sites. Would both of you briefly weigh-in on that issue?

Mr. STEINBACH. Yes, sir.

So we have engaged Twitter. We have spent lots of time discussing with Twitter our concerns but I think we need to be careful that—because what we do see is, like you said, individuals engaging in the public arena on Twitter and other social media accounts, but then they do very quickly take their conversations into private chat.

So on the public forums, or in the public arena, we see just conversation, First Amendment conversations, if you would like. So I would be hesitant to dictate to Twitter how to conduct its business. Now, we do have conversations with them and when it is appropriate we explain to them the threat and we would hope that, by the terms of their service agreement, they would then remove those posts. But for the most part, from my experience, what you see is individuals who quickly take the conversation offline to an encryption device or some other means to really discuss plans and really discuss those things that we would use to charge somebody with material support.

Mr. POE. Okay. I am about out of time so let me try to sum up just on this one issue.

Foreign terrorist organizations, though, are not—we are not permitted to help foreign terrorist organizations under the code that I just read to you. We would never allow ISIS to take out an ad in the Washington Post recruiting folks to go to Syria, radicalize, and come back and kill us. We wouldn't allow that to occur. Why? Because that would be aiding. To me, that would be violation of this statute. Statute does require, I am not talking about where we can disagree whether or not the recruiting. I am talking about open, obvious site of recruitment. Does the FBI, on occasions, recommend that Twitter take down that specific site?

Mr. STEINBACH. No, sir, we don't.

Mr. POE. So you don't make that recommendation to Twitter?

Mr. STEINBACH. No. What we do is if we see a site of interest, we provide them some type of process to start monitoring that site. Now, in many cases——

Mr. POE. They monitor it, or you monitor it?

Mr. STEINBACH. We request through legal process or through 2702, we request that we get access to stored content, current content, and then in many cases what ends up happening is, Twitter then voluntarily takes it down. But we don't——

Mr. POE. All right.

Mr. STEINBACH [continuing]. Specifically ask to take down a site.

Mr. POE. Okay. So you don't make that request. You let them make that decision on their own.

One more question if I may, Mr. Chairman?

The three individuals or four that were apparently arrested today, Coney Island, through public news sources, states that the information to find out who these individuals were was through confidential informants. I am not asking you to comment on that.

Confidential informants, as the term is used, is still one of the best ways, is it not, to find out who people are who are committing crimes not just in terrorism but any type of crimes in the community? Would you agree with that or not? Either one of you.

Mr. STEINBACH. Absolutely.

Mr. POE. Sheriff?

Sheriff STANEK. Oh yes, sir. We encourage it. Like you said, the ''See Something, Say Something'' campaign is akin to that as well.

Mr. POE. Thank you, Mr. Chairman.

Thank you, all.

50

Mr. GOHMERT. The gentleman's time has expired.

Now recognize the gentleman from Louisiana, Mr. Richmond, for 5 minutes.

Mr. RICHMOND. Thank you, Mr. Chairman. And thank you to the witnesses and we had a Homeland Security meeting going on at the same time, and I think that the protection of the homeland is very important to everybody and it has us scattering today.

Let me ask just a basic question. And, Mr. Steinbach, or Sheriff, you may have some insight. But, as you all deal and interact with ISIL, ISIS, IS, however you want to call it or the people involved in it, do you all have a sense of the endgame or what they perceive to be the win? And I ask that question because it helps me to understand, you know, how we deal with them in terms of homegrown terrorism and so forth.

So, Mr. Steinbach, do you have a sense of that?

Mr. STEINBACH. Yes, sir.

I think ISIL has been pretty outspoken in its plan to reestablish the caliphate. If you look at some of their open source information, the caliphate extends well past Syria and Iraq, it goes into Northern Africa, it goes north. So I think that is their stated intent. And so, when they look to recruit, they look to recruit lots of individuals, foreign fighters, professionals, to come to the caliphate to help establish that caliphate. And, if you can't come to the caliphate, attack the West.

Sheriff STANEK. Mr. Chairman and Congressman Richmond, I absolutely concur. I think that is, I mean, that is the answer. That is what they seek from us or to do to us.

Mr. RICHMOND. And I guess, in some of my reading and in it, I guess I was looking for the ultimate win and I don't know if it is the plan for the apocalypse or the end of the world or whatever, but part of that becomes then, what message are they using in terms of social media to people in the United States to get them excited about getting involved in this? So, is it true, just a push on the religion?

Mr. STEINBACH. Well, I think they have a very effective message. So, you know, perhaps previous groups like al-Qaeda identified the caliphate in years or decades to come.

Mr. RICHMOND. Right.

Mr. STEINBACH. ISIL has said the caliphate is now. Bring your family to the Islamic state now. And that is a fundamental difference. So it is a message that is resonating with a lot of individuals. And then, when you get online to some of these places, they describe a community, which is a false narrative of course, but they describe a community with schools and infrastructure and support services that I think younger and younger folks find attractive. And, again I will emphasize, that is a false narrative.

Mr. RICHMOND. And I think that is a consistent with everything that I have read, that they pushed, that there is free healthcare, there is free schooling, and that your food and everything will be provided for you, but if you still want to work and do exceedingly well. You can and, you know, to the extent we can, and to what extent have we made sure that we get the information out there that this is not true, that it is all propaganda—intended to suck

51

you into the cause and to get you involved, but it is absolutely not true.

And I have not seen that message out there as much as I have seen the opposite message.

Mr. STEINBACH. So I think you are right, sir. We have an effective counter narrative, but the volume, the sheer volume, we are losing the battle; to the amount of use of social media and other Internet-based activities eclipses our effort.

Sheriff STANEK. Mr. Chairman and Congressman, I think you are absolutely right, though. That counter narrative is really important and that is what we do when we counter violent extremism in our local community. When we reach out and work with the Diaspora community, they do it for us. We empower them. Like I said on, you know, Sunday afternoon, Sunday evening, after this video comes out about Mall of America and ISIL, the community itself responds. They didn't do that years ago. We have empowered them to be able to do that and work with them.

Mr. RICHMOND. Which is a great, I guess, probably last question is, how do we as a Congress and as a government empower them and include them more in helping us to fight something where we are at an adherent disadvantage as a government, as a traditional FBI or law enforcement, where minorities are so underrepresented? How do we expand the umbrella to help empower these and that faith religion to help us with this because they share our same interest and they want our same result, which is to defeat ISIS? So how do we include them?

And, Mr. Chairman, after that answer I yield back.

Sheriff STANEK. Mr. Chairman, can I answer that question?

Mr. GOHMERT. Yes, please.

Sheriff STANEK. Thank you very much.

Mr. GOHMERT. Both of you, if you wish, may answer the question; sure.

Sheriff STANEK. Congressman, I think you are absolutely right again. But, you know, should this Committee ever choose to get out of D.C., instead of you home districts, come visit me in Minnesota. I would be happy to sit down with you at the Safari Restaurant on 31st and 4th Avenue South, in the heart of the Somali community. Meet Abdi Warsame, a Minneapolis elected city council member, meet a member of the Minnesota legislature, the first one elected in the country. Meet the school board members who are Somalian Americans. Understand that they are working really hard and now they have moved on and now they are representing their community in the very venues like we do, like you do.

I think that is really important. And I encourage you, if you ever get a chance, call me. I would be happy to sit down and have a meal with you at the Safari Restaurant or somewhere else.

Mr. STEINBACH. And I strongly couldn't top that. I think the Sheriff is right. It is his efforts and the efforts of police officials and sheriffs around the country that need to be leading the way in this counter messaging effort. They know their communities much better than I do and I wouldn't pretend to take lead in that. I expect and it is happy to see individuals like this sheriff to take lead in that and make effective use of that outreach.

Mr. GOHMERT. All right. Thank you. The gentleman's time has now expired.

The Chair now recognizes a gentleman from Michigan, Mr. Bishop, for 5 minutes.

Mr. BISHOP. Thank you, Mr. Chairman. And I'd like to take the opportunity to thank both of you for being here today. It is refreshing to see the collaboration that goes on between local and Federal departments.

I am from the Detroit area, Oakland County, Michigan. Home of Mike Bouchard, who was our sheriff and has done a similar job in establishing a relationship with the Federal agencies in the Detroit area. And I am grateful for that because they are building the same kind of relationships. I was just briefed by the FBI in Detroit and they are doing a fantastic job.

In an area, we are a border community, we are a number of races, religions; it is a melting pot in our community. So it is a fulltime job in building relationships, and law enforcement has done a great job.

I mention that because ISIL controls a large swath of territory in Eastern Syria and Northern Iraq, and there are seven Nations that border Iraq and Syria including Iran and Lebanon. And near as I can figure, that is seven different exit points and entry points. And I am wondering if you can comment, I guess specifically to the director, do you have relationships with these foreign Nations the same as you have with your local law enforcement that help coordinate your efforts?

Mr. STEINBACH. So I wanted to say, just the FBI alone, the intelligence community, the U.S. government, has robust relationships with neighboring countries, Western allies, and that relationship has become all the more important as the world is shrunk in this speed with which information must be shared is needed. So, yes.

Mr. BISHOP. Thank you.

I want to go back to this "Going Dark" issue that you raised earlier. I didn't think you had enough time to expound upon that. As a former prosecutor myself, I understand the importance of information and having the opportunity to gain access to certain information. But I also understand the civil libertarians out there are concerned about how that information is accessed and the process by which you are to access it. We hear a lot of talk about Section 2702 and all these legalisms that are out there. But can you explain to folks generally speaking how you obtain this information and the fact that you just don't have open access to that information?

Mr. STEINBACH. Yes, sir. I would be happy to.

So I think it is important to note what we are talking about is not obtaining additional authorities, expanding authorities, but being able to use those existing authorities we have. So with the telecommunication and social media companies, the Internet companies, as they increase their technology, we don't have the ability to go in with the same legal authorities we have always had to obtain content. Whether that is a criminal investigation for child pedophiles or gangs or organized crime or terrorism. We are talking about going with a lawful court order, on the national security side of the house, that will be the FSK or, if we are talking about through the criminal side, through the courts, with a court order signed by a magistrate that would allow us lawfully to see that content.

We are not talking about looking in obtaining additional authorities or expanding our reach. We are talking about that same ability we have always had. And I will say that we are losing that ability. If you look at the numbers in a classified setting, we can talk more, but we are getting further and further away from that ability, that lawful ability that we are asking for.

Mr. BISHOP. Tell me, just so the public understands, what threshold that you have to show to gain access, to get that court order for example, to do what you need to do?

Mr. STEINBACH. So we have to go to a court, either the FISC or to a magistrate in the criminal courts or at the state level or at the Federal level, and show cause. So probable cause as to why, provide and affidavit that lays out the facts that shows why we believe it is important and necessary toward the investigation to look at that either that stored content in the search, or look at the ongoing content.

Mr. BISHOP. And a warrant is not issued unless there is an established probable cause based on the evidence you presented and the testimony you presented; correct?

Mr. STEINBACH. Correct.

Mr. BISHOP. Very quickly. There are three amendments to the Foreign Intelligence Surveillance Act which will be expiring on June 1, 2015, including Section 206 and 215 of the USA Patriot Act. Can you tell me how the expiration of these authorities would impact the FBI's ability to conduct investigations?

Mr. STEINBACH. I think it would have a negative implication. We use those tools responsibly, but we use them to identify those individuals that have stated an intent to conduct a terrorist attach or support a foreign terrorist organization. And if those tools, those lawful tools, expire, it will limit our ability to do our jobs.

Mr. BISHOP. Thank you, Mr. Chairman.

Mr. GOHMERT. Thank you.

This time, I will recognize myself for 5 minutes.

I appreciate you being here, your testimony. I am still confused after these years over communication problems within our homeland security. I wasn't here when homeland security department was created but, since I have been here at times, it seems like it has created more bureaucracy to get through in trying to get messages to and from the different departments that are affected.

I was curious. I had seen an article today, in Breitbart, about U.S. Customs and Border Protection and special agents with U.S. Immigration Custom Enforcement. Homeland Security Investigations got a tip about a large shipment of marijuana, it has resulted in finding a tunnel in a home in Arizona and it had a hydraulic lift coming up from the tunnel. They are saying 4,700 pounds of marijuana were found. And I am curious, the article indicates that a significant number of the finds of tunnels don't come from detecting tunnels.

Mr. Steinbach, are you familiar with efforts to try to locate tunnels that might be going across our border? I know it normally effects more the DEA but, ever since I read the Tom Clancy novel where, yeah, where the drug tunnels ended up being hired out by cartels, actually the Middle Eastern terrorists, I wondered if that isn't a possibility if some of our enemies are as smart as Tom Clancy was. Are you consulted? Does counterterrorism division look at those issues at all?

Mr. STEINBACH. We do, sir. And I think you break it down between known threats and vulnerabilities. So the southwest border would certainly be a vulnerability. So part of our job is working with the rest of the intelligence community, again, with the locals in that area, to discuss and research what potential vulnerabilities are out there that not only would be used by a drug cartel but could also be exploited by a foreign terrorist organization.

So we have a process. We work with our partners through the JTTFs, through the fusion centers, make sure that stuff like that, information like that, is spread horizontally across the infrastructure so that my folks in counterterrorism with a counterterrorism slant can look at it, the Sheriff's folks can take a look at it from local law enforcement. Really, the key is having an infrastructure set up so that the fusion centers, the JTTFs, have a robust information sharing process so that when stuff pops up across the spectrum of the 17,000 state and local and tribal agencies that it is quickly pushed to where it needs to go.

Mr. GOHMERT. You bring up the fusion centers. I had heard from some of our law enforcement that, gee, it has now become a one-way street, the feds want us to give them our information but we can't get information back from them.

Sheriff, how has your communication been in the last few months with the fusion center? Have you had any success in getting information from the Federal authorities?

Sheriff STANEK. Yeah, Mr. Chairman, you raise a good point as well. Some of that relies on individual states and your criminal intelligence sharing laws. Like, in my state, I am not allowed to share that information between Federal and local law enforcement. Many other states, it is some patchwork of local state laws.

However, we have a good relationship with our fusion center. Just on Sunday afternoon, we received a joint information bulletin from the FBI, from the Department of Homeland Security, talking about the Mall of America and this video that I referenced earlier. That is information we need. It was timely, it was accurate, it was to the point, and it helped us prepare or better prepare.

Mr. GOHMERT. And actually, you bring up, Mr. Steinbach, the issue of vulnerabilities. I had seen an article, February fourteenth, again Breitbart reported, that the border patrol agents catch Middle Eastern man sneaking into Texas and that is the most I had seen reported. But my sources indicate that actually he was from Iraq, he spoke fluent Russian, and that supposedly all he would say about his occupation is that he trained people. Does your counterterrorism division get word when people like that from countries where there is radical Islam at play, do you get word when those type of situations arise? Do you get a chance to question someone like—

Mr. STEINBACH. Yes, sir.

So I would say, going back to the fusion center piece, just to kind of show that type, we have over 100 agents and analysts sitting in fusion centers. We have got 57 of our fusion centers have access to FBI databases sitting there. That information starts generically at the local level and is pushed to us.

So in the case of the gentleman you are talking about, that would be classified as a ''special interest alien.'' Those individuals coming from countries of concern that need greater scrutiny to look towards, you know, what are their true motivations and intentions for trying to sneak across the border.

Mr. GOHMERT. Okay. Did you know about this particular Iraqi individual that trains people that speaks Russian?

Mr. STEINBACH. I, myself, did not personally.

Mr. GOHMERT. Okay. All right.

Well—yes?

Ms. JACKSON LEE. May I? I have just——

Mr. GOHMERT. I yield to the gentle lady from Texas.

You and I are the only ones left, so certainly. I doubt that since I would object that there is any other objection. So unanimous consent, you may.

Ms. JACKSON LEE. The gentleman is very kind. First, my appreciation to the Chairman for his steady line of questioning. We have worked together on a number of issues. And then, my appreciation. Mr. Chairman, I think you were here when I noted that Sheriff Stanek was here last week and was quick to accept our response, or our invitation to come back again to Washington. We know we might love it, and I am smiling with that, but we know that our visitors have work at home and we appreciate that.

We thank Mr. Steinbach for his years of service.

So let me just have these quick questions. I ask a question about women and the increasing recruitment of women and their adherence to extremism which has made a very big point in our meetings last week. So I want to make sure of that there is a different approach to how men are recruited and sometimes a different approach to women even though the practice is empowerment, excitement. Have you begun to look at that distinctiveness of the recruitment of women?

Sheriff Stanek?

Sheriff STANEK. Yeah, Mr. Chairman and Congresswoman, we have. In fact, I have had several conversation with a young Somali woman in Minnesota, very active, named Fartun Weli who serves on the sheriff's community advisory board. She is very engaged with the community. In addition, we meet roundtable of Somali women. Like I said, many of them are moms and they understand what is happening with their young people and what is driving and motivating them. They are the key at the end of the day to a lot of our outreach efforts with the community itself.

Ms. JACKSON LEE. So I will finish with Mr. Steinbach, but my final question to you is: You have been in law enforcement for 32 years and you were obviously serving during the heinous acts of 9/11, do you feel that we are better communicators and exchangers of information and intelligence today between local and state and Federal than we were pre-9/11 or 9/11?

Sheriff?

Sheriff STANEK. Yeah, Mr. Chairman and Congresswoman, I absolutely do.

You know, there was a time when we would have been at opposite ends of this table. Not anymore. Federal law enforcement agencies like the FBI and DHS are full partners with local law enforcement. I represent the Nation's sheriffs. I was impressed that the congressman knew Sheriff Bouchard who is my mentor, Sheriff Garcia from your county, and many of the others who serve here. We do it for the right reason every day, but we work hand-in-hand with our Federal partners. We may be the boots on the ground but we can not do it alone. We need what they have and they have been very willing, whether it is Director Mueller or Director Comey, to come to the table and provide that to us.

Thank you.

Ms. JACKSON LEE. Mr. Steinbach, I will finish the courtesies of the Chairman, first of all, thank you very much, Sheriff. First of all, to say that I would hope that if Congress gives Federal law enforcement more tools, such as for example, a thorough watch list and the no-fly list that we seek to make sure that it is thorough that that would be a helpful tool, even as it may be a large number or small number but always to be accurate, is a helpful tool. Is that not correct, Mr. Steinbach?

Mr. STEINBACH. Yes, ma'am. Of course. I think the more tools you can provide us, the better we are able to do our job. When you consider the evolving threat and the changing nature, I think the more tools are more important for us.

Ms. JACKSON LEE. I appreciate that.

Then, I would just ask you this simple question. I think you were certainly serving this country pre-9/11 and now you are continuing to serve the country. Would you say that the communication between all levels of law enforcement around this rising and increasing threat of terrorism is much better than it was when we couldn't follow the dots of a memo on a desk in, I believe, it was Minneapolis that did not connect the dots of individuals learning to take off and not land? Are we at a better point?

Mr. STEINBACH. I would say we are absolutely in a better place. And I will give you an example. From my perspective is, I don't have responsibilities necessarily for Minneapolis or Minnesota, yet I have met Sheriff Stanek on numerous occasions. We are not strangers. This is not the first time we have met. I have been at the major county sheriffs and major city chiefs. We have had interactions and we have a very robust relationship.

I think the JTTF process is the right balance of pushing and we have learned as we have gone. Certainly, we have made mistakes but we continue to improve. I would say that our information sharing process is better than it has ever been. And I would challenge us that we need to continue to not only share but share real-time, at the speed of light——

Ms. JACKSON LEE. I agree.

Mr. STEINBACH [continuing]. Because that is how quickly the information has to get passed.

Ms. JACKSON LEE. My last point: Would you reaffirm that the outreach tactics, relationships, with these unique communities, in this instance the Somalian community but there is the large populations in places like Michigan and elsewhere, Texas, is important and are you tune-in to the new element of extremism among women, particularly women that can be attracted to the fight with ISIL?

Mr. STEINBACH. Yes, ma'am. That tool is invaluable.

Ms. JACKSON LEE. Pardon me?

Mr. STEINBACH. That tool is invaluable. You know, when you look into radicalization, it is a spectrum. It starts with someone with intellectual curiosity and it drives to a point where they have developed an intent where enforcement disruption is necessary. But, before you get to the point where law enforcement action is necessary through prosecution, through deportation, there is a whole piece to that at the local level; the sheriffs is involved in and in trying to change that intellectual curiosity and change course of that individual.

Ms. JACKSON LEE. And women and extremism?

Mr. STEINBACH. Women and extremism, it is a new phenomenon and ISIL has taken advantage of it. They still are a minority but they are a much larger minority than they were 2, 3 years ago. And so, it is a new for us.

Ms. JACKSON LEE. Mr. Chairman, you have been very kind. I want to thank the Judiciary Committee and particularly this Subcommittee for recognizing its duty and responsibility. And the issue of extremism among young women is an issue of concern to me and I hope that this Subcommittee and the full Committee can look collaboratively on this unique but growing phenomenon that has a capacity to expand and become extremely dangerous.

So I thank the gentleman for his kindness. I yield back my time.

Mr. GOHMERT. I thank the gentle lady. The issue of communications was touched on eloquently. It brings to mind another couple of questions I wanted to ask Mr. Steinbach.

Previously, you know, numerous times we have had Secretary of Homeland Security here. And I have seen emails discussing, and they were not classified, discussing Secretary Napolitano's hands-off——

[Pause.]

Mr. GOHMERT [continuing]. List in reference to someone with known terrorist ties and that this individual, it turns out a man with known terrorist ties, foreigner, was on the secretary's personal hands-off list. Is your division ever consulted over people that, I don't know if I know Secretary Johnson has a hands-off list or not like apparently Secretary Napolitano did, but is your division ever consulted on people that may be put on a hands-off list by Homeland Security?

Mr. STEINBACH. So I am not aware of any hands-off list. I would say that we follow the intelligence, we follow the evidence. So if we identify information that suggests somebody is a member of supporting foreign terrorist organization radicalizing, we open a predicated investigation. That is a political move and we follow the intelligence to its logical conclusion. If that person is supporting a foreign terrorist organization, our job and our goal and our mission is to disrupt.

Mr. GOHMERT. Well, if someone is a member, associate of known terrorists, member of a terrorist organization, I would hope that your division would take notice of that. We had Secretary Napolitano testify and I asked her about a man, a foreigner, with——

ties, a member of foreign terrorist group, being allowed to visit the White House and she didn't know anything about it. She said ''I can live with that as long as somebody in Homeland Security knows about it and is vetted—''

[Pause.]

Mr. GOHMERT [continuing]. The individual and we had someone with those type ties that was cleared to visit the White House. Is the counterterrorism division ever consulted on people who may visit the White House who have ties to terrorist groups?

Mr. STEINBACH. Anybody coming to the United States is subject to a vetting process. The terrorist screening center, there is a multiagency process that reviews databases to ensure that——

Mr. GOHMERT. Are you talking about people coming legally into the United States?

Mr. STEINBACH. I mean, yes, sir.

Mr. GOHMERT. Okay.

Mr. STEINBACH. Yes, coming legally into the United States, there is a multiagency vetting process that reviews, to ensure that there are no ties that would suggest him or her a threat to the United States.

Mr. GOHMERT. Okay. So from that, do you know if counterterrorism division was consulted before a member of a terrorist organization was allowed to visit the White House?

Mr. STEINBACH. I don't know what incident you are talking about, sir, but——

Mr. GOHMERT. Okay——

[Pause.]

Mr. STEINBACH. I would say that the process isn't to contact counterterrorism it is to contact the terrorist terrorist screening center, to go through the database checks. We review that, we are apart of that.

Mr. GOHMERT. And whose duty is it to notify you that such a person may be coming to the White House?

Mr. STEINBACH. Any individual who comes to the United States——

Mr. GOHMERT. Right.

Mr. STEINBACH [continuing]. Is required to obtain a VISA, some type of legal process to come to the United States. Once they go to the State Department for that legal process, it kicks in a number of checks that are automatic regardless——

Mr. GOHMERT. Okay. Well now, that raises a whole other question because I understood the FBI was, I believe it was first the Russians notified the CIA that they had evidence or concerns that Tsarvaev had been radicalized and when nothing was done, as far as they could tell, they notified the FBI that they had concerns Tsarvaev had been radicalized, of course I am talking about the Boston Bomber. Are you now saying that counterterrorism division would have been notified by either the CIA or the FBI that the Russians had concerns that Tsarvaev had been radicalized or did you guys ever take a look at Tsarvaev before the Boston Bombing?

Mr. STEINBACH. So I think it is well-known, sir, that we opened a guardian based on information provided to us by that foreign government. At the end of the day, when we looked at the information, it didn't lead anywhere. And so, the guardian was closed.

59

Mr. GOHMERT. Were you aware of what investigation the FBI did before you closed that?

Mr. STEINBACH. Absolutely. There is a process before we close—
—

Mr. GOHMERT. Oh, I know. Director Mueller testified. They didn't go to the mosque to talk—they went to the mosque but it was under their outreach program. They never went to the mosque that was started by convicted terrorist Alamoudi to see if anybody there had any idea whether Tsarvaev had been radicalized, was he reading Qaeda, was he reading things that had been known to radicalize others? Nobody asked those questions at the mosque he was attending. And from what we can tell, the best we got from the FBI, they talked to the bomber and talked to his mother, but I never was able to get any other information that anybody else was really talked to thoroughly.

They talked to him, they talked to his mom. They say they are not terrorists, they go to the mosque and the outreach program, never asked about are there any terrorist-type comments, radicalized comments, has he read milestones like Osama bin Laden and is now thinking more radical. Apparently, nobody asked those questions, so I am really sorry, but it doesn't give me comfort that you would close it based on the testimony we have had from other individuals of how little they did to stop the Boston Bombing but we appreciate it.

And the record will be open for a period of—all Members will have 5 legislative days to submit additional written questions for the witnesses or additional materials for the record. And in fairness to both of you, if you think of something you would like to be part of the record, you would like for the Committee to know, than please provide that within 5 days and we will include that as part of the record as well.

Ms. JACKSON LEE. Mr. Chairman?

Mr. GOHMERT. Yes?

Ms. JACKSON LEE. I just want to acknowledge that I have a group of members who are former retired law enforcement and National Coalition of Law Enforcement Officers for Justice, Reform and Accountability who are in the audience. I just want to acknowledge them, the CLEO, and thank them for their presence here today.

Thank you, Mr. Chairman.

Mr. GOHMERT. Yeah, and I know we both share not only appreciate their presence but thank them for what they do day-in, day-out, so thank you for being here. Hearing nothing further, this hearing is adjourned.

[Whereupon, at 12:10 p.m., the Subcommittee was adjourned.]